L   cop.1

809.3   H29w
Harper
     World of the thriller

D1005805

THE WORLD OF THE THRILLER

The World of the
THRILLER

RALPH HARPER

The Press of
Case Western Reserve University
Cleveland / 1969

To
Howard Webber

PREFACE

I cannot recall a time, since I began to read, when I was not drawn to stories of adventure. Before I had finished third grade I knew Robin Hood and King Arthur so well that I played all their scenes with my friends after school. I was too timid to pretend to be Robin Hood; I think I was Will Scarlett. In my next period I exhausted the children's room of our public library, climbing the scale from tales of pioneers and Indians to Westerns. I still enjoy the latter in movie and television forms. And during one of the snowiest of New England winters I filled up my time reading and rereading the Rover Boys, the Boy Allies, and Tom Swift. By the time I reached high school I had graduated to the terror, if not the pity, of the detective story. From Edgar Wallace to Agatha Christie is a long day's journey, when it is filled with many of their popular colleagues; by the time I reached college I had made that journey many times. I have never been patient enough for the puzzles and games of this branch of the genre, however; I was attracted mainly by the heightened air of living which is engendered by danger. I still remember scenes from some of Mary Roberts Rinehart's books; she knew her places and people firsthand.

I do not think I read any spy stories—except for E. Phillips Oppenheim's *The Great Impersonation*—until my college days on the brink of World War II. Then I met a relative of Erskine Childers and was persuaded to read *The Riddle of the Sands*. Four years later I heard of John Buchan for the first time. It was a September day before term, and my moral tutor and I were passing Buchan's house at Elsfield, overlooking Oxford. I asked, "Who is John Buchan?" And he asked me in reply, "Haven't you read *The Thirty-Nine Steps*?" That was the origin of my predilection for spy stories.

I could justify this preference by saying that spy stories engage me more than detective stories. They are meant to, of course, but not more than Westerns. No, I believe that the spy story attracted me at a time when I was becoming obsessed by the fatality of Nazi cruelty and conquest, and instinctively I transferred my daydreaming from the kind of thriller that was intended to divert and entertain to the challenge of the contemporary political scene. I have never found the same mixture of sickness and menace in cold war novels. The rational crime, to use Camus' term, does not frighten me in the same way as the sick crime. The early spy stories still seem the best, except for John Le Carré's; but then he is a very fine writer.

No one is more conscious than I that if you are looking for connections between spy stories and other fiction you should mention Poe and Wilkie Collins, Gothic tales of all sorts, and above all the apocalyptic masters, Dostoevsky, Conrad, Kafka. But I have written of the latter elsewhere, and, in any case, I have something else in mind than a literary or sociological history of the thriller in general, or any of its branches. My interest is in the existential themes of the thriller and, more particularly, in the psychology of the reader's involvement. It is natural that one should want to make one's point as simply as possible, and for this reason alone it seems to me proper to illustrate my discussion almost exclusively from spy novels. In them all the salient features of the Western and detective story can be found, as well as a sensitivity to the fate of a far larger part of mankind, an entire nation if not the whole world. Here as in all kinds of thrillers a single man, a hero, has a chance to save, and with fortitude and intelligence.

The thriller can be taken as a philosopher's casebook, my kind of philosopher at least. My intention is to suggest a phenomenology, as it were, of reading thrillers. What is the nature of our involvement? What do we expose of our secret selves, our desires and ambiguities, our morality and idealism? What is the stream, the trouble, the pertinence of our inner life, as we find some "verisimilitude of satisfaction" in our reading? If I am right, the thriller's purpose is "transfiguration." For the brief time of reading a novel, we ourselves are sometimes transfigured; through the joint imaginative effort of writer and reader, we are placed in a world where we become what we really wish we were. This involves an act of dreaming on the part of those, like myself, who are inveterate daydreamers even without books, but who with the help of fiction can suffer a welcome sea change.

Perhaps the thriller is no more subjective in form than more serious fiction, but we feel that the author wrote it and expects it to be read in a daydreaming kind of mood. The reason we are sometimes embarrassed by an addiction to thrillers is that we would be even more embarrassed if we divulged the contents of our romantic pictures, our improbable fancies, and our vision of an absurdly improbable identity. In Dostoevsky and Kafka dream is nightmare, and the difference between nightmare and daydream is very important. It is a difference not so much between the past and the future—to tell the truth, some nightmares predict and warn of what may come—but between the involuntary and the voluntary, the subconscious and the more or less conscious. The problem of interpretation is different too.

There is a natural correlation between the existential categories in thriller plots and the existential concerns of the reader: the situations of crisis, danger, suspense, tension, terror, dread, in short, chaos and the absurd. Where there is violence and death there is also courage and resolution. So much is clear. But our more or less hidden hints of identity are not so obvious, the faces of man's interior world of discovery, the hoped-for poetic justice of all thriller fiction, and the recognition of tragedy in a world that has about given up on justice. A writer's sophistication can be measured by his awareness of the range of desire and endeavor, idealism and heroism, experienced by a complete man, and that man's fear that he is not yet complete.

Can the thriller bear the weight of such spiritual analysis? Why not? Its themes are weighty enough, even if their embodiment is not. Besides, what is improbable today? While I was writing the section "On the Run," one of my sons was himself on the run in Hué, during the Tet Offensive, hiding out in attics for eight nights and days. Anything can happen; everything does happen. More important by far than thriller plots is the reader's involvement. The thriller is one more place where millions of us meet ourselves at a level we are at pains to deny at other times. The ultimate question is, what is the connection between daydream and reality? Which is more real, which more fictitious? Or is there a third self compounded of both? For me, this question implies the answer.

RALPH HARPER
Monkton, Md.

CONTENTS

1

THE THRILLER:
Its World

The Place of the Hero

The whole world is the subject of the thriller, inner and outer, private and political, good and evil. All the sights and sounds, places and times, agonies and hopes are there gathered up, sometimes brilliantly. The many fascinating films that have been made from thrillers only prove that in the hands of a clever director even a second-rate story of international intrigue may become a plausible adventure in a plausible world. The thriller is concerned with a whole man's apprehension of this world as it appears in a situation of great crisis. The sights and sounds that are added to words by a movie effectively bring the totality of that apprehension into focus.

Some unapologetic reflection on the world of the thriller and the interior life of its readers is long overdue. Where spy stories alone are concerned, the genre has come a long way since John Buchan published *The Thirty-Nine Steps* in 1915. With that novel the spy thriller began its unbroken progress through the twentieth century. Erskine Childers' *The Riddle of the Sands* (1903) was its only real precursor, and bears the same kind of relationship to it as Pascal's *Pensées* to Kierkegaard's *Journals*, similar in form and content, but without immediate issue.

Graham Greene has remarked on the originality of Buchan:

> More than a quarter of a century has passed since Richard Hannay found the dead man in his flat and started that long flight and pursuit—across the Yorkshire and the Scottish moors, down Mayfair streets, along the passages of Government buildings, in and out of Cabinet rooms and country houses, towards the cold Essex jetty with the thirty-nine steps, that were to be a pattern for adventure-writers ever since. John Buchan was the first to realize the enormous dramatic value of adventure in familiar surroundings happening to unadventurous men.[1]

Already by 1940 there was no need to comment on the difference between Buchan and the detective story writers whose legendary hero was Sherlock Holmes. Conan Doyle's successful invention was notorious not so much because of his adventures as because of the infallible, even comical facility, with which he solved crimes. Holmes and Poe's Auguste Dupin set the tone for their successors: "As the strong man exults in his physical ability, so glories the analyst in that moral activity which disentangles."[2] Both uncovered and, in true psychoanalytic manner, exposed and left harmless the bizarre, the grotesque, the brutal, the ferocious. There is a vast difference, however, between the analytical emphasis of the detective story and the existential approach of the spy story.

Buchan, like Eric Ambler and Greene who followed him, was interested in a different world, the world of moral and political anarchy, a world in which evil cannot be restrained simply by analytical exposure. The human beings portrayed by Childers and Buchan are forced to contend against the powers of evil with their whole persons, not their minds alone. They must go down into the streets, be willing to cross continents and seas, risk their integrity and their lives. The thriller hero is the hero in classical and recognizable form. In a time when the anti-hero has been taking the hero's old place elsewhere in fiction, the thriller alone preserves him. All the strengths of man are displayed: stamina and courage, moral and political vision, and a sensitivity to persons as well as to the natural and technical world.

This is the reason why it can be said that the literature of the thriller might someday be turned to by historians who wish to see the shape of the world in the twentieth century: its language, customs, emotions, perils, people, and places.[3] Almost everything is there in some form or other in these popular archives of our time, even the music and architecture, and it is these features that often make it possible for the cinema to produce a silk purse from the sow's ear which some of these books are. There is something more: changes within the genre itself reflect important changes in the relationship of the individual to crisis. Just as the passing of the great detective, the fading of interest in tales of detection, and the rise of stories of international intrigue reflect the international dimensions of the modern conscience[4]— a watershed between centuries, less arbitrarily marked by World War I than by the year 1900—so the passing of the gentleman agent who was replaced by the professional reflects the widespread notion that international crises are too complex and too vast for any but an organization of specialists even to understand. The day of the amateur is over. In this age of general education, the specialist alone is trusted and hired to treat each of the many problems that modern man has to face.

It may be unfair to say that "competence replaces moral

stature as the criterion of the individual's worth";[5] the human symbols of John Le Carré's books, to say nothing of Greene's wartime books, prove that even the professional agent can be awakened to the moral aspect of his job. While Sam Spade may have had no private life, at least none of any significance to his work, James Bond, "cardboard booby"[6] that he is, creature of "M." that he is supposed to be, is always clumsily tripping over himself. If we know anything consistent about James Bond it is that he is James Bond first and "007" second. He is to be preferred to that insufferable egoist, Holmes, that spiritual eunuch who had to withdraw into the privacy of drugged dreams when his great intellect was not being usefully employed. Bond is not so superior to the rest of mankind that he has to show his contempt continually; on the contrary, he is saved again and again as much by good luck as by his own efforts, and one would be prudish and hard-hearted to deny him the appropriate reward of a simulacrum of love. Fleming at least paid lip service to the figure of the knight, chivalric and errant.

Vicarious Experience

What do readers wish for? There is no single and simple answer. Not even the usual one—escape. For while it may be true enough of "escape literature" that the reader wants to escape "real life," this is probably just as proper a motive for reading any kind of fiction and drama. For some people the everyday world is boring; for others, who also read thrillers, the everyday world is far from boring, and they do not wish to leave it for that reason. Sometimes very busy, responsible people leading lives of high tension admit that they read thrillers to relax rather than escape. But how can one relax if he has only exchanged one kind of tension for another? Many do, and we must look first at the shape of the fictional tension in order to understand this.

Admittedly, life is boring and fatiguing to a great many people, and not all of them get any satisfaction or excitement out of thrillers. Edmund Wilson is not the only person who is bored by all thrillers.[7] Too many people who cannot write well think they have found in the thriller an easy way to make money. All they have found is a way to add to readers' exasperations. The thriller writer does not really lead a privileged life, no matter what the lending libraries say. A bad thriller is worse than other bad writing, shoddier, and if we read the first page of a great number of thrillers it is because we hope to find in them certain satisfactions that we do not find in our everyday world.

Vicarious experience may not be as good as real experience. But it is a lot safer and cheaper. Compare the cost of a Caribbean vacation with the price of an Ian Fleming paperback. It is different in other ways too. Morality aside, and Dr. No and Honeychile Rider, few of us would choose a life of tension so explosive. Why then do so many choose the same tension vicariously?

One answer comes to mind immediately. A world of vicarious experience does offer the satisfaction of having a beginning and an end. So much of life is not satisfying, even when not boring, only because it is always unfinished. Except in some deliberately open-ended works of the imagination, most fiction and drama represent experience as unified, in time and in fulfillment of intention. If life seems boring, part of the reason is that it also seems unending. Even when life is unbearably tense, from pain or responsibility, part of the reason is that one cannot let go. When we read thrillers we do let go, not only of the tensions that strap us, but of the finale as well. One way or another there is a resolution, either a final episode to the course of events, one that sums up the whole course, or a discovery of the meaning of the events. In a real world, where there is all too often neither meaning nor finality to look forward to, even vicarious experience is a welcome change.

Justice and the Absurd

If thriller literature is typical of the twentieth century, it is because of its content not its form. We do not usually think of thrillers as examples of new or experimental writing. On the contrary, most thrillers observe the oldest rules of the fiction game and show a fondness for poetic justice. In a world where so much either does not come out right or threatens not to, it is pleasant to bathe our cynicism in an imaginary world where we know at the beginning of the story that the side we are on will prevail. Naturally we have to assume that anti-Communist or anti-Fascist thrillers would not be popular with those for whom they are not intended, Communists or Fascists. Indeed, the thriller has been frowned upon in totalitarian countries (only now is it coming to life in Russia). Since the thriller has some regard for truth and justice seen from the perspective of a free mind, it can be judged positively subversive in some political climates.

If this were all that need be said about the world of the thriller, we could define it properly as the very opposite of what Camus called "the absurd," i.e., the disjunction between the nostalgia for justice and unity on the one hand

and the unreasoning silence of the world on the other. There is no question but that the thriller represents a taming, a simplification, and a setting to rights of the most serious evils and perils, and it does so in a manner which revives our confidence in a misused and discredited humanity, by the coincidence of luck and virtue. As readers, at least, we can rejoice at a display of competence we ourselves do not possess, and vicariously enjoy encounters with timely good fortune. More than competence, we get a special satisfaction from representations of total commitment. When crises rise to a climax, instead of dragging on as our own do, a combination of competence and commitment richly deserves a break in fortune that every thriller reader anticipates from page one. Sooner or later all will be well, all manner of things will be well.

And yet just as we would be remiss to overlook the importance of poetic justice in the thriller, we would be even more remiss to be silent about the chaos that is the streambed and the stream of every kind of thriller. Finally, we understand that the definition of a thriller must include two judgments of reality that are usually kept apart: poetic justice and the absurd. It is when evil or the threat of evil undermines our confidence in the natural and social order, and the reader is shaken up, that the thriller gets off to a good start. Whenever a writer fails to persuade his readers to take evil seriously, he cannot expect the readers to care whether justice is done. Just as too much sex or too much violence can, believe it or not, be boring, so can too many international intrigues. "Here we go again," we say, and put the book down. We had hoped to be presented with a fresh situation. We wanted the nature of the situation to be evil in such a way that we could believe it. We must first be shocked, and shocked so that we can be reassured. No, this is not quite true; we also sometimes want to be shocked because we need to be shocked out of lethargy and complacency. The Greek tragic dramatists knew this well, and Aristotle wrote more profoundly than we sometimes give him credit for, when he said that tragedy evokes pity and terror. A certain amount of terror is good for us, and instinctively we seek it, but without tears.

The "shocker" is the mass media's imagination of the absurd, making credible the chaos which the champions of justice and gentleness will successfully control. It is the popular counterpart of existentialist philosophy, as Guido de Ruggiero pointed out so contemptuously more than twenty years ago.

There is something in existentialism which excites the imagination with the morbid curiosity of the thriller. For the heavy, somnolent categories of traditional philosophy, it substitutes new and imaginative symbols: Incarnation, the wager, pre-occupation, anguish, the leap, shipwreck, etc. which give to the happenings of our everyday world a turbid, romantic sense, at once attractive and repellent. The analogy with a thriller can be pushed further; in both cases there is an intermingling of elements which become more complicated and entangled as the story proceeds and which create in the mind of the reader a sense of the spasmodic, evergrowing tension, but which then quite unexpectedly collapses like a great blister when it is pricked by a pin, and the inanity of the epilogue resolves the preceding tension.[8]

This is not the place to comment on his contempt for existentialism, except to admit that the analogy is fair so long as we are thinking of the similar involvement of the reader in the complications of reality as represented. In all too many thrillers, however, the epilogue is inane, and one wishes the writer had had sense enough not to push poetic justice too far and tidy up all loose ends into one banal ball of fluff.

Banality and Humor

Perhaps this fear of banality lies behind the predilection some writers (notably Chandler and Deighton) have for a pert repartee that barely escapes being sick. Indeed, Harry Palmer's wisecracks in the film version of *The Ipcress File* and *Funeral in Berlin* help to establish and then support a tension that the thin plots could not otherwise provide. Undeniably the contrast between the nonestablishment figure of Harry Palmer in situations that represent the struggle between establishments of almost cosmic proportions, is quite satisfying to those of us who would like to be able to treat the cold war in the same offhand manner.

"It's going to be very difficult for me if I have to answer questions as I go along," I said. "If it's all the same to you, Minister, I'd prefer you to make a note of the questions, and ask me afterwards."
"My dear chap, not another word, I promise."
And throughout the entire explanation he never again interrupted.[9]

Who of us does not want to be listened to? The wish seldom lets us speak so candidly. Harry Palmer's model was Philip Marlowe:

I sat down on a pink chair and hoped I wouldn't leave a mark on it. I lit a Camel, blew smoke through my nose and looked at a piece of black shiny metal on a stand. It showed a full, smooth curve with a shallow fold in it and two protuberances on the curve. I stared at it. Marriott saw me staring at it.

"An interesting bit," he said negligently, "I picked it up just the other day. Asta Dial's Spirit of Dawn."
"I thought it was Klopstein's Two Warts on a Fanny," I said.[10]

There is room in the thriller for humor, as for almost everything else. Would that there were also room in existentialism. Room for pertness, cockiness, and also for parody. Perhaps parody did not appear for the first time in Fleming's novels, but it certainly turned up in the movies made from his books. As soon as Bond speaks his lines, nonchalantly and complacently, the contrast with their desperate situations is too much for us. Graham Greene made the most of this in *Our Man in Havana*, his parody of Fleming. The thriller will never be the same again, and it will be hard to pick one up without automatically preparing to read an imitation of an imitation. To tell the truth, the world of the thriller is always playing with opposites that are seldom found together. We need a stronger dose of the plausible to make our vicarious experience of the implausible believable.

The Implausible and the Improbable

It always takes a sure touch to prevent the melodramatic from dissolving into the ridiculous. Theoretically, there is no reason why the implausible should not occasionally happen. In the abstract there is no reason why God should not appear to men, but it is unlikely. In thrillers the implausible not only happens all the time, as the hero is offered an opportunity to right wrongs or to stem the tide of chaos, but the almost impossible also happens—the hero succeeds. When you put two such implausibilities together in a hero like James Bond, the formula bursts. Even so, when the fantastical is also the absurd, in Camus' philosophical sense, and the hero is a person with believable characteristics, an amalgam of endurance and self-reflection, an inheritor of appropriate skills and a child of fortune, then all the elements of the actual and the dream world meet to contrive an imagined resolution of anarchy. Greene, in referring to his "absorption with failure, pursuit, and poverty," his "fixations," admitted that for him they "could best be expressed in the melodramatic, the contemporary and later the Catholic novel."[11] Accordingly, when we wonder why anyone should be interested in the implausible, it might be because readers as well as writers have their fixations, and they include all the diverse elements that make up the world of the thriller.

The writer, however, is usually more self-conscious about his motives and basic concerns than the reader. What is a fixation to the writer may rather be the mode of operation of the reader's unconscious, his "primary world," to use J. R. R. Tolkien's phrase. For many adult readers the thriller, like the fairy story for children, offers chances for "fantasy, recovery, escape, consolation." The double meaning of fantasy applies to thrillers, the subjective mechanism of projecting one's desires and anxieties, on the one hand, and the artistic projection itself, the verb and the predicate, on the other. There is no essential difference between the thriller bought at the airport and the daydream back home. The main difference would be the clothing of the same anxieties and desires with someone else's physical world. We do get tired of our own thinner and repetitive plots, and the written word of another person adds a note of external confirmation to an inner and private experience that is so peculiarly our own. Of course, there is a problem of identifying ourselves in some way with the subjective experience of our literary or film counterparts, and this cannot always be done. When it can, the placing of the counterpart in Berlin or Scotland, with an appearance so different from our own, different past and different job, adds a verisimilitude of satisfaction to the identity of anxiety and desire. This is, in short, what we mean by vicarious experience: objectively no experience at all, yet subjectively one and the same as the hero's.

As if the vicarious experiencing of the absurd were not enough, the implausible or fantastical is often tacked on or inserted. For the absurd is not the same as the implausible, nor is fantasy the same as the fantastical. Sometimes a sense of probability is stretched and strained; and at other times we accept the improbable with exhilaration, so eager are we to exchange the life we know for the life we would like to know. *The Thirty-Nine Steps* is a series of improbabilities, from Scudder's murder in Hannay's flat to the latter's discovery at the last moment of the thirty-nine steps. But who cares? The entire plot belongs to a "primary world," and within that world of national crisis, heroism, and perseverance, the romantic pitch of total commitment never falters. This is Buchan's response to enforced bed rest, Hannay's chance for relief from boredom, and the reader's attachment to an adventure where the stakes are high and where he alone can be depended on to succeed. Dorothy Sayers was probably speaking mainly of her own Peter Wimsey stories when she said, "We read tales of domestic unhappiness because that is the kind of thing which happens to us; but when these things gall too close to the sore, we fly to mystery and adventure because they do not, as a rule, happen to us."[12] She might just as well have been thinking of Buchan's adventures of Hannay and Leithen. They do not happen to us, it is true. Is that the reason, however, why we turn to them?

Or do we turn to them because they match our own daydreams? In *The Ministry of Fear* Arthur Rowe, an unheroic man, sees our world (also Dorothy Sayers') differently: " 'It sounds like a thriller, doesn't it, but the thrillers are like life—more like life than you are . . . you used to laugh at the books about spies, and murders, and violence, and wild motor-car chases, but, dear, that's real life: it's what we've all made the world since you died.' "[13] No doubt Buchan's world did sound laughable, and entertaining, in the twenties; but by the thirties the Nazis and Communists had changed all that. Even the surface of life began to resemble the world of the thriller. Anything can happen to anyone at any time. Nevertheless, most of us still do not expect it to. We go on making the old distinction between the probable and the improbable, the actual and the fantastical, secure in the expectation that things will remain the way they are. We do not anticipate being asked to carry secret documents to a secret rendezvous, with the outcome of our journey deciding the destiny of millions. No, we do not and probably will not, but we can enjoy the fantasy of pretending.

A New Mythology

The writer of a fairy story has no scruples about playing fast and loose with plausibility. Grimm's "King of the Golden Mountain" is hardly more implausible than *Goldfinger*, and however improbable it is that the fisherman's wife Ilsabil could become either Emperor or Pope, her excessive greediness ("for my wife good Ilsabil wills not as I'd have her will") is not unknown in the real world. The thriller writer does have scruples, at least to the extent of providing a more detailed rendering, only up to a point sometimes, of the factual world. In more sophisticated thrillers, those by Childers, Greene, Le Carré, realistic characters are set against a realistic background, and only the situation out of which the plot evolves is unusual or unlikely. Even there, as Greene has noticed, one can expect almost anything today. What then is left, if the implausible is withdrawn? Only the threat of the absurd provoking the best in the hero and reader? Stripped to essentials, the thriller does not need either a superfluity of facts (as in Adam Hall's or Len Deighton's stories of professional agents) or outsize villains (like Drax, Red Grant, or Mr. Big), or sexpots with outsize breasts (like Honeychile Rider, Vesper Lynd, or Pussy Galore), accomplishing Herculean fun and games. What the thriller does need is a grasp of the "primary world," or, to say it more plainly, an appropriate myth.

This can mean different things. The writer can consciously make use of mythology, only decently covering myth in modern dress. Or he can use it unconsciously. As David Ormerod and David Ward have suggested, one way to read Fleming's novels is to enjoy his use of "ancient myth as a quarry for the easy realization of his spectacular fantasies."[14] It is true that Fleming's books, more than most, are especially open to Freudian analysis:

The reader is to be entertained by an externalization of his deepest fears and fantasies—he is to be given the chance, through the hero, of vicariously enduring every attempt by the hated father-figure to maim and destroy him, and is at last to kill the father and enjoy a substitute for the mother, whom he must at last cast off out of respect for the real mother. He is to enjoy the love of a brother, who must yet be mutilated or die before the action is completed. He is to be equipped with a license to kill, and released from anxiety about his sexual fetishism by being given a gun by the good father, a figure in whose service Bond commits all his unlikely acts of violence and sexual self-justification.[15]

Bond's obsession with sex and violence makes this sort of interpretation quite plausible. Even so clean a story as Geoffrey Household's *Rogue Male* can be read as a take-off on the Oedipus story. The transgressor is hunted by a father-figure and is immobilized in the womb of mother earth. He kills the father with an arrow. Carry on, Freudian reader. If this makes sense, then why not see Richard Hannay as some kind of transvestite?

However comical or enraging ready-made readings are, and how boring literature becomes as each text is stamped with the same Freudian interpretation, no one can be prevented from seeing analogies between fiction and myth. The more important question is whether these analogies matter, and whether fiction may not produce new myths occasionally, as Franz Kafka has for us. In the case of the thriller, the primary world is the soul's perpetual struggle between good and evil, between virtue and chance, desire and satisfaction, gentleness and violence, and each memorable piece of fiction becomes a new vehicle, or myth, for it. In one of the earliest of spy stories, Childers' *The Riddle of the Sands*, characterizations and background are as authentic as in any succeeding novel. It is a comforting book, a healthy minded story of two young Englishmen in the years before 1914, cruising in a centerboard boat over the tidal sands of the north German coast, uncovering the beginnings of a German plan to invade England in seagoing light-ers. No better story has ever been written about small boat sailing, and it is also recognizably a thriller, combining "a life of toil, exposure, and peril," with "a secret so important and delicate." Davies and Carruthers are a perfect match for this life and their "riddle of the sands," for they have all of Richard Hannay's earnestness and sincerity without his self-praise and snobbism. What they are worth they show rather than tell, and compared to Buchan's heroes, who are self-consciously virtuous, they are set apart from imitation gentlemen by their "sensitive reserve"[16] and by "a humility born of acute sensitiveness to [their] limitations."[17] Granted that their pre-World War I perils were not as crude and devastating as those before, during, and after the second war. The ingredients of the "primary world" are clear enough: love of adventure, a patriotic struggle against the forces of evil, an opportunity for individual heroism, and, even here, the prospect of reward by love as well.

Gentlemen and Pros

Whether we interpret a thriller from the viewpoint of mythology or philosophy, as a Freudian or an existentialist, it is only right to take notice of certain obvious features of the thriller's history and topography. The spy novels them-selves are divided between those authors whose heroes are gentlemen and whose adventures take place outdoors (Childers, Buchan, and Household), and those whose heroes belong to the urban world and have professional or semi-professional careers, and who do not as plainly belong to what Household complacently calls "Class X." "Who be-longs to Class X? I don't know till I talk to him, and then I know at once. It is not, I think, a question of accent, but rather of the gentle voice."[18] Perhaps so, but I feel sure that Bernard Shaw would rejoin, "Balderdash, of course, it's a question of accent." Overlapping the distinctions between country and urban, gentleman and journalist or business man, is the more recent distinction between civilian and professional, the man who becomes an agent by chance, and the man whose livelihood depends on his profession. After World War II the typical hero of the spy story was the trained official of the British Secret Service or the American Central Intelligence Agency.

This suggests a digression. America has produced many novels of espionage, but no outstanding ones. The British have had a corner on this part of the thriller genre from the beginning. Is it because so many Englishmen with literary inclinations and talent have at one time or another worked for one of the security services? Or is it rather that the cold war is more abstract to Americans, and we are satisfied more easily with stock characters, stock situations and plots, and the similar rhetoric that we hear from TV? Dashiell Hammett and Raymond Chandler, the best American thriller writers, developed styles to express the native struggle against violence.

From Childers to Greene there is a similar pattern of involvement and development of adventure. Nowhere is the nature of the involvement clearer than in the semi-autobiographical *Ashenden* by Somerset Maugham: "Ashenden, a writer by profession, . . . chanced soon after his arrival to go to a party and was there introduced to a middle-aged Colonel whose name he did not catch. He had some talk with him. As he was about to leave, this officer came up to him and asked: 'I say, I wonder if you'd mind coming to see me. I'd rather like to have a chat with you.' "[19] From then on Ashenden was hooked. How casual, how unexpected, and how desirable. This is the way it works in daydreams. The self is needed, wanted, invited, and from then on becomes the center of adventures on which depends the fate of many nations. That Ashenden must remain anonymous and will not even be thanked for his successes, that most of his work will be routine and more boring than his profession as a writer, is irrelevant compared to the privilege of being lifted out of a private life into a life with international dimensions.

All the so-called classic thrillers—all, that is, until we reach the ones with pros as heroes—begin as casually and unexpectedly. One day a man leads a humdrum life, the next he is inextricably swept into someone else's crisis that has complications both perilous and secret. The peril initially involves a small circle of conspirators and their opponents, and at the same time must be kept hidden by both sides. Sometimes the hero must attempt to live in both worlds at once; sometimes he is forced to drop out of sight, partly to stay alive, partly to carry on his battle against the powers of darkness. Hannay (the expansive side of Buchan) and Leithen (the more inhibited side), Ambler's Latimer and Kenton, Greene's Rowe and D, all leave civilian life for secret adventure by chance. How else could one expect the dream mechanism to work? And yet, chance is not simply a mechanism; it is also an important ingredient of the actual world, even if it does not usually present opportunities as exciting as in fiction.

The Classic Pattern

The classic pattern of plot was set once for all by Buchan

in *The Thirty-Nine Steps*, and even the more recent tales of professional espionage only add unessentials. Out of boredom, through some chance encounter with a world where things are really happening, where the stakes are big and life is lived at high tension, a man hunts and in turn is hunted, is trapped, caught, escapes, and finally defeats his enemy. Suspense there may be in a detective story, but only in a spy story, sometimes called a "chase" story, is the hero's own peril always central. If the plot of a detective story is sensational—and most are not—the horror or scandal is evoked by the events which the hero observes, rather than by his own predicament. When the detective himself is threatened, his peril simply reinforces the general gravity. The secret agent on the other hand, whether amateur or professional, becomes involved and therefore integrated into a world completely different from his own, and he will not be released until that world is made harmless, temporarily if not finally. In the Bond novels, for example, the chief villain sometimes escapes and is encountered again later in another book. But organizations like Spectre and Smersh do not disappear as long as Russia needs them. Ernst Blofeld is foiled in Switzerland and Nassau only to be squashed finally in Japan. A thriller can hardly lay claim to being a thriller if it does not bear this initial distinguishing mark of the spy story: the vulnerability of the hero. Not only can he be hurt badly; once involved, he can never be an observer again until his side has won.

This accounts for the atmosphere of restlessness that is characteristic of thrillers. In the detective story the detective gives the criminal no peace, and of course the nearer he gets to exposing the criminal, evidence, and motives, the greater the risks he runs that, because of his despera-

21

tion, the quest will backfire. Compared to the secret agent, who from the beginning of his involvement merges with the world of his enemies, the detective is secure and has the leisure and peace of mind that are needed for his inquiry. The confidential agent, on the other hand, also inquires, but from within the ranks of an enemy who is already, wholly or in part, identified. More often than not, confidence is offered to both sides at once, and the hero becomes a double agent, a pretended ally of the very enemy he is trying to foil or destroy.

This approach means that he will have to take on a new identity, and it is only a question of time before his disguise wears thin and his real identity is uncovered and he is trapped. The hero had already taken a new identity when he walked out of his normal life and assumed a new and, from the reader's point of view, desirable role. When he submerges his new identity in the disguise required for penetration into the confidence of the enemy, his peril is only heightened in the reader's mind by the fascination which he (the reader) instinctively feels before the instability of these two new identities covering the man as he once was. It is difficult enough for most of us to be assured of our ordinary identity these days; when two other identities are superimposed, even vicariously, the challenge to our hold on truth is exquisitely intense and demanding.

The variations of the classic pattern are not important, but they freshen the attention of the aficionado. Not for that reason was torture introduced in the spy novel for the first time by Eric Ambler. He was only reflecting one of the main differences between the World War I climate of John Buchan and the Nazi-Communist world of the thirties and forties. No one gets beaten up in Buchan, although Edward

22

Leithen on one occasion, in *The Power-House*, fears he will be when he sees some ruffians closing in on him. From Ambler to the present, ruffians do more than close in, and the hero barely escapes with his life. We have come to expect physical and mental pressure and injury to the extent that a relaxed spy thriller would seem a contradiction in terms. In fact, so much punishment is given out that the author has no choice but to invent a hero who is abnormally tough. The result is that the cold war hero can no longer be a man just like us, but must be trained to take terrible punishments which would kill or demoralize the rest of us. This is one reason why the British spy story has been willing to learn from the "tough school" of American fiction, particularly from Hammett, Hemingway, and Chandler. The international world since the thirties has been so much rougher than Buchan's world that only the tough can hope to survive. The loss to fiction, however, has been considerable.

The Real World

Graham Greene's figures stand somewhere on the line between these two sectors of contemporary history. They live in the new world threatened successively by Nazis and Communists, yet they are not really fit for these worlds. Greene does not submit them to the more outlandish tortures that Fleming inflicts on Bond. Arthur Rowe had lost his memory after a bomb explosion, but, far from demoralizing him, this gave him the rest that his conscience needed in order that a capacity for love might be restored in him. *Confidential Agent* opens with D being pummeled by a chauffeur bigger and stronger than himself. Wormold alone comes out unscathed from his dalliance with a real conspiracy. In making fools of his own secret service, which took his faked reports of enemy rockets in Cuba seriously, he provoked the enemy into taking him seriously too. This parody of Bond takes one back to Joseph Conrad's *The Secret Agent* and the lazy anarchist Verloc, who also finds one day that more is expected of him than routine reports. Conrad, like Greene, could see the ridiculous in the banal, the secret agent in the shopkeeper, the stupidity and ineffectuality of secret services. They both knew what the public is only now beginning to understand, that espionage establishments exist in large part to cancel each other out.

There are people who like the game of spying for its own sake. Kierkegaard once said, "My only desire at one time was to be in the police. It seemed to me a fitting occupation for my sleepless intriguing mind."[20] Many thousands in each of the major countries, and hundreds in all the others, are paid to do what they enjoy doing most, ferreting out the secrets of other people. Most of what they gather is in the public domain already, and only needs a computer to record it. Except for the political dimensions of the information, the secret agent's curiosity is not essentially different from that of country gossips (but these amateurs are more harmful, and they take themselves more seriously). Conrad's Verloc, for example, was a "famous and trusty secret agent, so secret that he was never designated otherwise but by the symbol Δ in the late Baron Stott-Wartenheim's official, semi-official, and confidential correspondence."[21] Verloc, in short, was a fool in a company of fools.

Kierkegaard was not a fool, and he immediately realized that the real police, real spies, did not offer him a fitting occupation for his sleepless, intriguing mind. "I imagined that among criminals there were people worth fighting with, clever, crafty, desperate men. Later on I recognized that it was a good thing I gave up the idea; for almost everything the police have to deal with is concerned with poverty and misery—not criminals or gangsters."[22] This is why the atmosphere of Conrad's novel is so drab and sordid. It is also why Kierkegaard instinctively found his vocation elsewhere, "a spy in the service of the highest."[23]

Not even in fiction are all spies in the service of the highest. Many authors take pains to present professional agents whom the reader cannot warm up to. Grodek, the master spy in *The Mask of Dimitrios*, Control in Le Carré's stories, M. in Fleming's books. Nor does the reader want his espionage hero to be true to life. Indeed, it is almost coincidental that there are confidential agents in fiction and confidential agents in real life. The true nature of the former is to use, as it were, the profession of the latter as a cover. The kind of human being that the thriller writer is interested in and that readers identify themselves with is a fuller and more complicated being than what can be normally understood under the cover of secret agent. The fictional hero who is plunged into more risks and more perils than the run of the mill intelligence officer is at least intended to be a complete man.

The Complete Man

Marshall McLuhan by no means exhausts the possibilities of the thriller hero by summarizing his characteristics as (a) individualism and lonely pride, (b) worldiness, (c) multifarious but specialized learning, and (d) passion for action and excitement, although he does suggest the reason why this hero is universally admired.[24] There is something in him for everyone. He is a very private man who is used to privacy; he is self-reliant, proud, and at home with self-reflection. He is always honest, candid, and loyal, a man of honor. Put all this side by side with a sustaining energy above the average, and we see the basis for his resilience, even toughness. Combine toughness with individualism, and we know how he can function anonymously, not needing recognition as much as other men, and not wanting any notice that can impede his job or his quest. He cannot be ignorant or innocent but must know his way around. Open to the secrets of the world, he is vulnerable; he is one to whom things happen. They happen to him, and they happen to others when he is near. His existence guarantees excitement and explosions. Evil is attracted to him as flies to flypaper. But with the innocent and gentle, natural victims of this world, he is himself gentle, chivalrous, full of compassion. No wonder he is attractive to women. His integrity is complete.

This thriller hero, figment of the imagination of twentieth-century man, is given adventures whereby he can unravel or cut the embraces with which the evil octopus threatens to strangle mankind. If he is a detective, like Oedipus, he will try to solve the riddle of the sphinx, or the sinister ambiguity of some oracle. If he is a hunter of men, like Oedipus, he may hope to identify himself with the life of his time, interrogating without fear or favor, until he has found the man who has brought death and sickness to mankind. Sometimes he will find, like Oedipus and Latimer in *The Mask of Dimitrios*, more than he bargained for. Sometimes he may even find, like Oedipus and the spokesman for Class X in *Rogue Male*, his very own self.

Setting out to arrest evil, he will find in the course of his efforts that he himself is on trial. At times he may be tempted to take the advice of Tiresias: "Leave well enough alone—why stir up dirt and make everyone unhappy."[25] But he cannot; it is always really too late. And so, as Chandler has put it, "Down these mean streets a man must go who is not himself mean, who is neither tarnished nor afraid. . . . He is the hero, he is everything. He must be a complete man and a common man and yet an unusual man."[26]

Do we identify ourselves with him because he is a common man, or because we delight in seeing a common man who is unusual? "He must be the best man in his world and a good enough man for any world."[27] The genius of the writer is to avoid making his hero display all his virtues with equal splendor, and yet at the same time all the virtues must be active in him. The result is that each protagonist, if not each author, exhibits one feature of "the complete man" more demonstrably than the others. Le Carré's Smiley, for example, "was one of those solitaries who seem to have come into the world fully educated at the age of eighteen. Obscurity was his nature, as well as his profession. . . . A man who, like Smiley, has lived and worked for years among his country's enemies learns only one prayer: that he may never, never be noticed."[28] Sam Spade does not mind being noticed; what he does mind is having anyone prevent him from doing his job. " 'This is my city, and this is my game.' " " 'When a man's partner is killed, he's supposed to do something about it.' " " 'I won't play the sap for you.' "[29] His integrity is his loyalty to his job, and not even love can shatter that. Compared to him, Le Carré's John Avery is a little boy playing agent. His wife sees this clearly:

"You've been telling me people don't matter, that I don't, that agents don't. You've been telling me you've found a vocation. Well, who calls you? Are you a martyr? Should I admire you for what you're doing?"
"It's nothing like that. I'm doing a job. You want me to say double-think, don't you?"
"No, you've said what I want you to say. You've got to draw a circle and not go outside it. That's not double-think, it's unthink."[30]

By the time John Avery has grown up it is too late—a man he has trained has been sent into East Germany and done all the wrong things and got caught. There is nothing left to do but cry, and he does. Sam Spade was not playing at being detective, and he never undertook what he was not capable of carrying through himself.

Not only does the hero have "an immense energy and a gift for organization, no scruples, but resource, courage, and determination," he can be expected to put aside everything secondary in order to do his job or carry out his mission. In this sense, if no other, he is honest. Sometimes he is honest all the way through. " 'You are D. I know you are D. If you aren't honest, then the whole putrid world . . .' "[31] But the trouble is that "trouble is [his] business,"[32] and he becomes the focus of evil wherever he walks. " 'He says you are not as smart as you think you are, but that you are a guy things happen to.' "[33] "The nightmare was back: he was an infected man. Violence went with him everywhere. Like a typhoid-carrier, he was responsible for the death of strangers."[34] Of course, this is not meant literally. To say that he is infected is not to say that he is sick. To say that he is responsible for the deaths of others, apart from killing in self-defense, is not to say that he is a criminal. Far from it, the thriller hero is not rotten to begin with, and he need not deteriorate. He does get very weary and cynical.

Philip Marlowe could be speaking for all the other private eyes and confidential agents when he says,

"You don't know what I have to go through or over or under to do your job for you.[35] . . . The first time we met I told you I was a detective. Get it through your lovely head, I work at it, lady, I don't play at it.[36] . . . I'm a very smart guy. I haven't a feeling or a scruple in the world. All I have the itch for is money. I am so money greedy that for twenty-five bucks a day and expenses, mostly gasolene and whisky, I do my thinking myself, what there is of it: I risk my whole future, the hatred of the cops . . . I dodge bullets and eat saps, and say thank you very much, if you have any more trouble, I hope you'll think of me. I'll just leave one of my cards in case anything comes up."[37]

One thing is certain, the fictional detective or agent is not in the business for money, not even if he is a professional. He plays the game for its own sake, like James Bond, or, like most thriller heroes, because he has some sense of social responsibility. He may not always be able to articulate his motives; like Leamas in *The Spy Who Came in from the Cold* or the "I" in *Rogue Male*, he may not even know his motives until the action is almost over. In fact, he may be presented to the reader as an embodiment of the fundamental "decency" which for many Anglo-Saxons is always associated with the morality of "our side."

Talk of "decency" too often reveals the stupidity, hypocrisy, and self-righteousness of a side or a person who has no more right to claim moral superiority than his enemy. Even when admirable, it may refer only to a negative morality, such as, "I didn't mean to hurt him." At best, more is meant than that. It can ring changes on the great virtues of sympathy and compassion, self-sacrifice, and a sense of justice:

the just man justices;
Keeps grace: that keeps all his goings graces.[38]

The just man does not have to talk about justice, and if he does talk about justice too much we are apt to suspect cant. This is not to say that the thriller hero is a strong silent man who can be depended on to do the right thing instinctively. He may be very articulate, but about everything else than his own beliefs; not only does he have no time for that, he is not usually in search of a spiritual resting place. " 'What sort of person was I?' " asks Arthur Rowe. And he is told, " 'You had a great sense of pity. You didn't like people to suffer.' "[39]

Unfortunately, people do suffer in thrillers, and the best of the heroes become sad, world-weary men. In this respect there is a vast chasm separating the unflappable cheerfulness of most of the well-known fictional detectives— Maigret, Poirot, Perry Mason, and others—from Philip Marlowe, Arthur Rowe, Leamas. Even John Buchan, as he grew older and had to try to assimilate the shattered, unstable post-World War I years, lost the boyish ebullience of the Hannay of *The Thirty-Nine Steps*. Hannay himself never seems to have changed, but his world did, and perhaps this is why the quieter, more sophisticated Leithen began to replace him in Buchan's affections. At some point the thriller hero begins to realize that life will never be the same again, that even when this adventure is over, he will always be on call. What began by chance and was accepted as an interlude, gave the hero new obligations and a new understanding of what goes on in the world. In the end, there are no amateurs, only pros. Hannay and Leithen, Rowe and D, and the English gentleman who stalked the dictator, have been translated, so to speak, to a plane of existence that they were not intended by training or profession to function in. Their view of life will be conditioned forever by this translation; their courage, convictions, and endurance will always be at the disposal of the victims of terror. Unlike James Bond, they will not ask for assignments. They know too well, and they dread, the ruthlessness and rottenness of the powers of darkness. As Marlowe put it, "I looked down at the chessboard. The move with the knight was wrong. I put it back where I had moved it from. Knights had no meaning in this game. It wasn't a game for knights."[40] Not for damsels in distress either. Somebody has to rescue them, and so the knights try, at least in fiction.

Villains

James Bond rescues the damsel Solitaire from the big, bad Mr. Big. Like Philip Marlowe, Bond prefers "smooth shiny girls, hardboiled and loaded with sin," even if they sometimes take you to the cleaners, as the cop says to Marlowe. And Fleming himself seems to have preferred villains like Mr. Big, who, as John Pearson has observed, have "precisely the qualities that children most fear in adults."[41] "All demonstrate the threat of extreme physical power which an adult presents to a child, and their sadism contains that element of fearful irrationality which a child detects in the cruelty of an adult."[42] There are two kinds of villains in the Bondiad: the independents like Dr. No and

Drax, who are also megalomaniacs, and the organization villains like Le Chiffre and Ernst Blofeld, who are sadists. Seen by a "cardboard booby" they are as bogeymen to a little child, a Mardi Gras grotesque.

In John Buchan's world, evil is represented in a rather adolescent form, the adolescence of an English boy brought up on the pompous romanticism of *The Boy's Own Paper*. The awareness of evil is sentimental, vague, telling more about the boy's sense of duty to kill the dragon than about the character of the dragon. The descriptive emphasis, as in Bond, is on size. "He had told me something which sounded big enough, but the real thing was so immortally big, that he, the man who had found it out, wanted it all for himself."[43] Whether it is Germany on the rampage or "the Power-House" (Promethean iconoclasm), the simple-minded hero and his equally simple-minded friends tremble with virtue and indignation as they acknowledge the presence of the unthinkable in their midst. Noblesse oblige, patriotism, school spirit run amok, and it is only a question of time, not luck, before they step on the dragon. *Rogue Male* was written within the same tradition. It takes the hero an astonishingly long time to realize that he wants to kill the dictator, and when he understands his motives they turn out to be simple and respectable: the Nazis had murdered the girl he loved. When he admitted his obsession with this, he "declared war upon the men who could commit such sacrilege."

From Evil to Evil

Not until Eric Ambler began writing in the late thirties did any degree of sophistication about the powers of darkness enter the thriller. And even then his perspective is, from our point of view, rhetorical and simplistic. In the thirties there was still more than a touch of Buchan in Ambler's sentimental assertion that "it's not just a struggle between Fascism and Communism, it's between the free human spirit and the stupid, fumbling brutish forces of the primaeval swamp."[44] The context of this passage is threatened torture. In fact, it is in *Background to Danger* that torture makes its delayed entrance into the spy story. Ambler's books reflect the stages of contemporary conflict, from the early days of Fascism and Nazism to the cold war.

In *Background to Danger* also Ambler displays for the first time in thriller literature a critical attitude toward capitalism. Buchan had been establishment-minded. Big Business was good, and most of its leaders were gentlemen who were deeply concerned about the future of mankind. Even the villains were gentlemen, brilliant establishment members not quite right in the head. Buchan had no use for socialism and felt that "the young entry" was not all it used to be. He would have castigated Ambler's insistence that "at some point in the business structure there is always dirty work to be done."[45] "International business may conduct its operations with scraps of paper, but the ink it uses is human blood."[46] Ambler himself was a little ashamed of such emotionalism. Indeed, he points out in *The Mask of Dimitrios* that "Latimer as an Englishman could never quite overcome his distaste for other people's rhetoric . . . he had recognized one or two phrases as coming from the Communist Manifesto."[47] Nevertheless, Ambler's antipathy toward Big Business was consistently expressed in novel after novel, and he shared the view of young English intellectuals in the late thirties that "political ideologies had very little to do with the ebb and flow of international relations. It was the power of business."[48] Consistent with this is his sympathetic treatment of the Soviet brother and sister spy team, Andreas and Tamara Zaleshoff. One would never know that that comic heavy Zaleshoff was an agent of the same country that employed Rosa Klebb and Red Grant. The writer's point of view makes all the difference. It is the voice of the writer Latimer in *The Mask of Dimitrios* and the point of view of Zaleshoff (in *Background to Danger* and *Cause for Alarm*) that pronounce so solemnly, "My curiosity about D. was that of the biographer rather than of the detective . . . I saw him not as a corpse but as a man, not as an isolate, but as a unit in a disintegrating social system."[49]

Philip Marlowe's business is investigating disintegration, and he sees it more personally and categorizes it more plainly: "Trouble is my business." He is at his best and fiercest when he spews out his feelings about Carmen Sternwood: "A pretty, spoiled and not very bright little girl who had gone very, very wrong, and nobody was doing anything about it. To hell with the rich. They made me sick."[50] "I looked her over without either embarrassment or ruttishness. As a naked girl she was not there in that room at all. She was just a dope. To me she was always just a dope."[51] Even when he found her for a second time in his bed, naked, he remained bored until she called him a filthy name. Then followed an outburst more startling in its frustration than anything else in Chandler:

I didn't mind that. I didn't mind what she called me, what anybody called me. But this was the room I had to live in. It was all I had in the way of a home. In it was everything that was mine, that had any association for me, any past, anything that took the place of a family. Not much: a few books, pictures, radio, chessmen, old letters, stuff like that. Nothing. Such as they were they had all my memories. I couldn't stand her in that room any longer.[52]

And when he had thrown her out he "tore the bed to pieces savagely."[53]

Carmen Sternwood was mad, but no less rotten for that. The charming Austrian Hilfe (*The Ministry of Fear*) was mad too, but in a different and much more dangerous way. Like other Nazis he was attracted to nihilism, "not caring for anything, having no rules and feeling no love."[54] He believed in employing "the maximum of terror"[55] to rule the earth. The reader, like the thriller hero, instinctively knows where he is with such an enemy, and it is easy to decide how to feel about him. But Greene himself knew all along that the division of good and evil is never simply a geographical matter. In the earlier *Confidential Agent,* D believes in his cause and yet admits that his side commits atrocities too. " 'I've chosen certain people who've had the lean portion for some centuries now.' "[56] When asked whether his leaders are any better than his rival's he says, " 'No, of course not. But I still prefer the people they lead—even if they lead them all wrong.' "[57]

This is a clean world compared to the one John Le Carré writes about. It is probably the same world of professional espionage that Maugham described so unemotionally: " 'Of course, a lot of nonsense is talked about the value of human life. You might just as well say that the counters you use at poker have an intrinsic value, their value is what you like to make it; for a general giving battle men are merely counters and he's a fool if he allows himself for sentimental reasons to look upon them as human beings.' "[58] So speaks

Colonel R. to Ashenden, and forty years later we hear the outraged replies, which Ashenden is too much of a stick to make himself, in John Le Carré's *The Spy Who Came in from the Cold* and *The Looking-Glass War*. There is a difference now. Not only do the security services of each country sacrifice their agents for the sake of winning—who speaks of a Cause any more?—they sacrifice them also for the sake of doing-in a rival service. The serio-comical effort of Leclerc's almost defunct service to regain its wartime fame by putting an incompetent agent over the border into East Germany, is stopped by the intervention behind the scenes of Control, Leclerc's successful rival. When Smiley, Control's right-hand man, suddenly suspects that his chief had given Leclerc rope to hang himself, his dismay is ill-received: " 'Goodnight, George,' Control said; and fiercely, as if he were tired of sensibility: 'Run along. And preserve the difference between us: your country needs you. It's not *my* fault they've taken so long to die.' "[59] But it is Smiley who must take the news to Leclerc waiting at the border to hear from his agent. " 'We're disowning him. It's never a pretty process. He's as good as caught already, don't you see?' "[60] It is over, despite Avery's hysteria—for he had trained the victim to trust him: " 'You can't do it. You can't just leave him there for some squalid diplomatic reason.' "[61] It is worse than that; he is sent and he is left because he is a pawn in the rivalry of two security departments of the same government.

In a world where more and more officials believe their end justifies using other people as means, after a while nobody really cares about the means any longer, and when it is mentioned at all, it is only in tired slogans. The work of the professional agent does not encourage a concern for individual

human beings but only for what the old pro, Leamas, finally admits is nothing but "an operational convenience." He
had been used, sent into the enemy's land as a double agent,
ostensibly to expose and destroy the head of the enemy's
secret service, only to discover that it is precisely that particular man who has to be preserved because he too is a
double agent. By the time Leamas has realized what is going on, and everything works out as Control planned, Leamas has helped to destroy an enemy he has come to respect,
and has fallen in love with a girl who will be killed because she knows too much. Angry and sick over what he
has helped to contrive, he cries out:

"They used us. . . . They cheated us both because it was
necessary. . . . There's only one law in this game. . . . What
do you think spies are: priests, saints and martyrs? They're
a squalid procession of vain fools, traitors too, yes; pansies,
sadists and drunkards, people who play cowboys and Indians to brighten their rotten lives. Do you think they sit
like monks in London, balancing the rights and wrongs?"[62]

He who had been unwilling to argue his Cause with Fiedler,
the Communist he had come to respect, now says: " 'I don't
believe in anything . . .—not even destruction or anarchy.
I'm sick, sick of killing but I don't see what else they can
do . . . everywhere's the same, people cheated and misled,
whole lives thrown away, people shot and in prison, whole
groups and classes of men written off for nothing.' "[63] Liz,
to whom he is speaking, will soon be one of them.

The development of a moral sense in the history of the
thriller may not have reached its end yet, but it must have
reached some kind of climax. When it has become impossible or irrelevant to distinguish between the morality of
one side and the morality of another in the cold war, it is

37

high time to ask what has happened to Complete Man. The answer is plain, he has lost his vision of ends. As J. Bronowski says in *The Face of Violence*, "The good are as much out of hand as the bad."[64] The only way to distinguish the good from the bad is to call ourselves good and to call the others bad. We should not be so surprised at the course the thriller has taken; it is only reflecting the course of contemporary history. From the start of the detective story as well as the spy story, the pursuit of justice has taken place outside the law. The private detective is the hero, not the police; in fact, the police are usually pictured as inimical, jealous, or corrupt. The detective has to be willing to break the law, like a peace or civil rights demonstrator, in order to right wrongs which society and its officials are too stupid or too indifferent to right by themselves. Similarly (and we see this in Childers and Buchan) the gentleman hero, strictly amateur and civilian, does not trust the competence or the concern of the official counterintelligence services. Whatever competence they have is nothing compared to the intuition of these amateurs, whose attitude is, as Bronowski puts it, "The law is an ass."[65]

All this is tantamount to saying that the thriller hero experiences the excitements of a criminal while still retaining the reputation of an honest man. We should be curiously hypocritical if, while enjoying exposing the moral ambiguity of the thriller hero, we forgot that he is our hero. If he is ambiguous, so are we, his creators and readers. We ought to be sophisticated enough to know—if not honest enough to confess—that the world of the thriller is our own world, interior as well as exterior.

2

THE THRILLER:
Its Categories

Situational Fiction

If a thriller does not get off to a good start, it is usually a dud. No other work of fiction depends so heavily on mood and situation. The thriller is situational fiction. When it is advertised as a novel of manners (Dorothy Sayers) or a novel of ideas, an "eschatological thriller" (Anthony Burgess' *A Tremor of Intent*), the definition of the genre has been stretched too far. The true thriller aims to involve the reader's feelings in the situation, and the reader, if he wants to read thrillers at all, wants to be involved, and resents being misled.

The Thirty-Nine Steps begins with matter-of-fact reminiscing of the start of a long chase: "I returned from the City about three o'clock on that May afternoon pretty well disgusted with life."[1] The reader anticipates that he will not be bored. As Richard Hannay is about to enter his flat, a man with "small gimlety blue eyes" appears at his elbow and begs to be let in. He stays overnight, hiding from mysterious enemies who are seen waiting in the street below. The next morning his host finds him "lying sprawled on his back . . . a long knife through his heart which skewered him to the floor." Buchan was not a great stylist, but he knew how to keep a reader's interest from flagging. His formula was to let the hero be chased until he was caught, and then give him a chance to break loose.

How differently *The Mask of Dimitrios* begins: "A Frenchman named Chamfort, who should have known better, once said that chance was a nickname for Providence. It is one of those convenient, question-begging aphorisms coined to discredit the unpleasant truth that chance plays an important if not predominant part in human affairs."[2] At this point a reader might fear he had begun an essay, but if he keeps going a little, he sees that "the story of Dimitrios Makropoulos is an example of this. The fact that a man like Latimer should so much as learn of the existence of a man like Dimitrios is alone grotesque. That he should actually see the dead body of Dimitrios . . ." By this time the reader is engaged by a cleverly balanced mixture of situation and reflection that is characteristic of Ambler at his best. At his worst, as in *Background to Danger*, the reader can only wince and hurry past: "One sunny morning in July, Mr. Joseph Balterghen's blue Rolls-Royce oozed silently away from the pavement in Berkeley Square, slid across Piccadilly into St. James's, and sped softly eastward towards the City of London."[3] Fortunately, Ambler was a fast learner, and whatever defects his later books had, they were not defects of style.

Opening lines are indications of the point of view, the narrator's degree and kind of involvement. The casual self-deprecating tone, so self-consciously British, of *Rogue Male*, covers more than gentlemanly reticence and fair-mindedness; in this case, it covers a subtle, complex mind that finally explodes and then is integrated by a deep-seated desire for vengeance. The opening lines give no inkling of the denouement, only of a mind unwilling to make hasty and self-centered judgments: "I cannot blame them. After all, one doesn't need a telescopic sight to shoot boar and bear; so that when they came on me watching the terrace at a range of 550 yards, it was natural enough that they should jump to conclusions."[4] We are with the man with the rifle, overlooking someone on a terrace.

We are not there, however, when Ian Fleming begins *From Russia, with Love* with an equally simple, visually focused scene: "The naked man who lay splayed out on his face beside the swimming pool might have been dead."[5] It is an effective beginning, and we are immediately interested. But we are not "there." Why? Because, as elsewhere in Fleming, descriptions of situations are given to us for their sensational value. This is the major attraction of the Bond stories, and it is no wonder that Fleming himself grew tired and bored after several years of having to dream up one sensational situation after another. It is like living on drugs and wishing one did not have to. He was capable of something else, as we can see in the first paragraph of *Casino Royale*: "The scent and smoke and sweat of a casino are nauseating at three in the morning. Then the soul-erosion produced by high gambling—a compost of greed and fear and nervous tension—becomes unbearable, and the senses awake and revolt from it."[6] The description is economical; Fleming got it right because he knew casinos. He did not know firsthand what it is like to have his testicles slapped by a carpet-beater, but any man can imagine that. If he failed to become the good writer that he longed to be, and to write the spy story to end all spy stories, it was in part because he could not resist showing off.

The very flatness and dullness of the beginning of *The*

Spy Who Came in from the Cold provides the right setting for a sad, quiet, and cynical man and the story of his discovery of the worthlessness of human life: "The American handed Leamas another cup of coffee and said, 'Why don't you go back and sleep? We can ring you if he shows up.' Leamas said nothing, just stared through the window of the checkpoint, along the empty street."[7] Leamas' silence is all that is needed to make for suspense, and this most carefully constructed of thrillers never lets the reader down, right up to the last lines, where "they finally shot him, two or three shots. He stood glaring around him like a blinded bull in the arena." How much he had gone through between the checkpoint and the Wall, how intricate the maze of deception that was finally revealed to Leamas and to ourselves. Le Carré's special gift for gently turning the screw without letup is displayed once again in *The Looking-Glass War*, in the tranquil, lyrical opening and the echo in the finale:

Snow covered the airfield. It had come from the north, in the mist, driven by the night wind, smelling of the sea. There it would stay all winter, threadbare on the grey earth, an icy, sharp dust; not thawing and freezing, but static like a year without seasons.[8]

.   .   .   .

The farmhouse lay in darkness, blind and not hearing, motionless against the swaying larches and the running sky. They had left a shutter open and it banged slowly without rhythm. . . . They had gone, leaving nothing behind them but tyre tracks in the hardening mud, a twist of wire, and the sleepless tapping of the north wind.[9]

They had left nothing behind them, only one dead victim of their pretend-game, and one demoralized conscience.

It is a relief to pass from the sobriety and tragedy of Le

Carré to the smart and cynical flamboyance of Chandler. Marlowe is cynical about his job, but not about mankind. Even though Le Carré is the profounder of the two, there is place, the place of comedy, for the tough jauntiness of Marlowe. For as in slapstick itself Chandler forces his hero to endure the beatings and humiliations that only a rubber doll or Marlowe could take without demoralization, so that this man can protect the old, the innocent, the failed. To survive is to succeed, and only one who can make us laugh could survive:

It was about eleven o'clock in the morning, in mid October, with the sun not shining and a look of hard wet rain in the clearness of the foothills. I was wearing my powder-blue suit, with dark blue shirt, tie and display handkerchief, black brogues, black wool socks with dark blue clocks on them. I was neat, clean, shaved and sober, and I didn't care who knew it. I was everything the well-dressed private detective ought to be. I was calling on four million dollars.[10]

After a while the comedy becomes a mannerism, like a tic, and we feel Chandler, like his admirer Fleming, growing weary of the effort to turn out smart lines. In the end it is an effort to read them. Neither Fleming nor Chandler wears well, unlike Greene, who, however self-conscious his metaphors and similes, unfailingly reminds his readers of the moral landscape of pity and mistrust that his "entertainments" make so real. In the midst of life there is death. In the midst of homeliness there is the grotesque. In the midst of innocence there is always a victim: "There was something about a fête which drew Arthur Rowe irresistibly, bound him a helpless victim to the distant blare of a band and the knock-knock of wooden balls against cocoanuts. Of course this year there were no cocoanuts because there was a war on."[11]

THE WORLD OF THE THRILLER

Crisis Literature

In the thriller there is always a war on or a war about to go on. The same seems true in some detective stories, on a smaller scale. Perhaps it is not a question only of scale. The detective, at worst, has but to fear seeing the murderer's (or the gang's) victims struck down one by one like nine little Indians; he never has to bother with the fate of nations. There is a limit to the number of people one criminal can destroy, unless like Drax he controls the Bomb. This is the reason why secret agent stories are the touchstones of thriller literature; they represent evil unlimited. It is not accidental, therefore, that the thriller should thrive in the twentieth century. As Greene has put it, "Reality in our century is not something to be faced."[12] T. S. Eliot had already observed, "Human kind cannot bear very much reality."[13]

And so it is not simply situations that the thriller presents dramatically and concretely, but crisis situations. Thriller literature is crisis literature, and has arisen in the same century as a crisis theology and an existential philosophy, as a response to the crises of our civilization. What readers find in these books is not abstract analyses either of turmoil or of mores, but a pretense at firsthand, on-the-scene experiencing of the heart of the matter, the nuclear human matter. Of course, it is not really firsthand, not on-the-scene at all, although reality is just as strange and just as dangerous as fiction. Most people never live in the focal eye of national crisis, and only in their reading of thrillers do they feel they are participating in operations from the command post.

Readers come to thrillers, whether they know it or not, with quite different expectations. Some like their crises sensational, and their heroes splendid and brave. Others are prepared for—what to many would be distasteful—a spectacle more discouraging and sordid: " 'I thought life was much simpler and—grander. I suppose that's how it strikes a boy . . . [but] . . . all this talk of . . . Hitler . . . your files of wretched faces, the cruelty and meaninglessness. . . . It's as if one had been sent on a journey with the wrong map.' "[14]

The world is full of wretched faces, cruelty, and meaninglessness, and some thriller writers show that world to us, and we are actually grateful to them, for we would rather know the truth about ourselves than be entertained by a boy's dream or an adolescent's sensations. Civilization is as precarious as a night-blooming flower that closes when we switch on the greenhouse light. " 'Did you ever reflect, Mr. Leithen, how precarious is the tenure of the civilization we boast about?' "[15] So John Buchan in *The Power-House* in 1916. No, Mr. Leithen had not, until he was involved in a plot to upset it, and Buchan was only recording the astonishment and disillusionment of millions who had discovered in those early years of the war what the whole world has not been able to forget since, namely, the flimsiness of the very best and their vulnerability to destruction by the worst.

The End of Our Time

We do not live in a Manichaean world, with absolute and absolutely separate powers of good and evil. But at times we do not resist the temptation to think so. Individuals go astray, and nations are taken over and corrupted by the frustrated and unrestrained. Sometimes it is the good people themselves who, out of weakness, make it possible for evil to have its way. Indeed, the really bad man always has power and usually some grain of better sense, which if channeled differently could have helped to make a better world. The world that he does make appears to the thriller reader first as a conspiracy. Buchan saw this too. "Civilization is a conspiracy . . . modern life is the silent compact of comfortable folk to keep up pretences."[16] Then one day someone lifts the slab and we see the squirming slugs. The thriller puts this in concentrated, but also endurable, form. Fortunately, most of us do not have a chance to be involved in dangerous adventures; we are not up to handling them, and we know it. In no time at all we would be demoralized and not have enough presence of mind to learn anything from immersion in such adventures except to wish we had never met them. Nevertheless, there is much to learn that is both sobering and inspiring in the crises around us with which we are personally unfamiliar. The thriller provides us with a cheap and easy way to correct any inclination we may have to judge that all things, all manner of things, are well. Nicolas Berdyaev, just a few years after Buchan started writing, was saying, "Nowhere and in no single matter is solid earth felt underfoot, we are on volcanic ground and any eruption is possible, material or spiritual . . . we are entering into a realm of the unknown and the unlived, and we are entering it joyously and without much hope."[17]

We may discount his pessimism, but most of us would say—perhaps mistakenly, from a self-centered perspective —that we live in a constant state of crisis, politically and emotionally. What Berdyaev called "the end of our time" is a way of expressing a sense of being hung up on a watershed in history; it is also a way of making an eschatological point. We fear final catastrophes. There is so much evidence at hand for all to see, without reading novels, of general instability. One of Buchan's most readable books, *The Three Hostages*, was written after World War I and contains several impressive commentaries by a country doctor, Dr. Greenslade, about the demoralizing aftereffects of that first conflict. He speaks of " 'the amount of stark craziness that the War has left in the world,' "[18] and goes on to say that " 'a large part of the world had gone mad, and that involved the growth of inexplicable and unpredictable crime. All the old sanctities [have] become weakened, and men [have] grown too well accustomed to death and pain.' "[19] Much the same kind of comment has been made during the last twenty years also; we can only suppose that mankind can be exposed to just so much carnage and legalized murder before the ship of sanity really does begin to break up. Already we have seen one of Buchan's predictions come to pass: "Let there come a time of great suffering or discontent, when the mind of the ordinary man is in desperation, and the rational fanatic will come by his own."[20] Buchan was anticipating the spate of planned violence that Camus was to call rational terror and rational crime.

In this respect the grotesque, nightmarish figures of evil —otherwise comical—in Fleming's series of adventures are versions of the loose-screw political and military fanaticism of these decades. We do not begin to understand them until we listen to their inhumane logic. How well Dostoevsky prophesied the things that were to come, even better than Nietzsche. When man ceases to believe in God, all things are lawful. In fact, it would be a good thing to do a little evil in order to prove that all restraints are removed, and man can now replace God if he wants to. If such a man, having no illusions or restraints, is moved by pity for poor, stupid, suffering humanity, let that man organize life so that, at some slight price, mankind can be made happy. At any price? At the price of more misery. "How big and desperate the thing is that we are up against," said Buchan;[21] yes, and crazy too. So "how are you going to write detective stories about that kind of world on the old lines?"[22] The answer is, you cannot. But Buchan kept on trying, and although he retained his ability to keep the reader's interest moving from page to page as his heroes, now hunters and now hunted, are swept up into the chase, his figures of evil remained essentially unfrightening, and club men in their inevitable defeat. Buchan could not understand the demonic and the sadistic; his mental world was too romantic and optimistic. There was something Edwardian about him: a Scot, not to the manner born, he admired an England that was vanishing. In all his writings he showed a fascination for lost causes. Success had come quickly to him, and he extolled the Roman virtues of the English public school products long after it should have been apparent that the modern world was too labyrinthine and unstable to accommodate either Cicero or Seneca.

The new world, our present world, was understood and represented far more accurately by Franz Kafka, whose *The Trial* was written about the same time as *The Three Hostages*. Kafka, of course, was writing from middle Europe, and he was a Jew. Without being intentionally prophetic, Kafka was obsessed by the absurdity of life, an absurdity foretold by Dostoevsky and Nietzsche, and finally nailed down and stamped by Albert Camus. The new psychological world—its political counterparts were yet to come— Kafka had felt as a hidden and malevolent Law hovering over unwitting man, who looks for justice and finds none, not even poetic. It has taken forty years for thriller literature to catch up to Kafka.

Boundary Situations

Thriller literature is situational literature, crisis literature. In the language of Karl Jaspers' existentialist philosophy it is the literature of boundary situations. Man is always in situation, but only occasionally for most men is life reduced to total questionability by any particular situation. Jaspers, following Kierkegaard, suggested that there are a few special situations like those concerning death, fate, guilt, and major choices that bring individuals to the boundaries (border, frontier) of their lives, and where they must decide what they want to live by. Paul Tillich's schema of existential anxieties is a systematic (and more subjective) working out of Jaspers' suggestion: the anxieties of death and fate, guilt and condemnation, meaninglessness and emptiness (each pair containing an absolute and a relative threat). The plots of thrillers, unlike novels of manners, ideas, romantic love, travel adventures, are principally designed to illustrate such critical situations.

This is why even in a poorly written thriller, as most are, it is possible for the author to capture the reader's complete attention at some point, generally at a point where the many elements of someone's life are reduced to the alternative of a complete stop or a new turning. Only rarely is this grasped abstractly, in metaphysical terms—Greene comes as near to this as any—but rather in terms of naked choice of the most simplified and self-canceling alternatives. One choice means death or the collapse of our personality, the other means life, literally life, in which we shall never be the same again.

The situation never allows us much time to choose. From day to day decisions can be deferred without disaster; in fact, the normal rule by convention, habit, and imitation means that it is very rare for a radical change of direction or belief to be made at all. Sam Spade's story in *The Maltese Falcon*, of the man who suddenly left wife, job, and town one day, and never returned, is the story of a man who acknowledged the opportunity of a boundary situation and tried to live up to its warning. A beam had fallen off a building, just missing him as he walked along the sidewalk.

"He was scared stiff, of course, he said, but he was more shocked than really frightened. He felt like somebody had taken the lid off life and let him look at the works. . . . He said he knew before he had gone twenty feet from the fallen beam that he would never know peace again until he had adjusted himself to this new glimpse of life. By the time he had eaten his luncheon he had found his means of adjustment. Life could be ended for him at random by a falling beam: he would change his life at random by simply going away."[23]

He moved from Tacoma to Spokane, got a new job, a new wife, and bred new children. In the end nothing was different.

This is what usually happens. Dostoevsky told the story of his own near-execution on the Moscow parade ground, and his last minute reprieve. When he thought he was going to die, he told himself that everything would be different if he were allowed to live. When the reprieve came, life seemed so miraculous that he was sure he would go on seeing everything anew. A week later life was just as it had always been. So most of us recover from the shocks and ills of life, grateful to be alive, positive that our sense of the freshness of reality will remain joyfully concentrated. But it does not. Only rarely does a new vision or some new value remake our total outlook. We know and regret this, perhaps only instinctively in most persons, and, out of something deeper than curiosity, are drawn toward what we hope will be the more complete experience of crises that we find in thrillers.

On the Run

Here is where, if we are alert, the thriller lets us down. The curious thing is that we do not know we have been let down most of the time. The characteristic thriller experience of crisis is being "on the run." Every aspect of this experience is described in great detail—all, that is, but one, the inner apprehension. And yet this is precisely what makes it a definitively different kind of experience. Either the writer does not know this firsthand, or he assumes that as the reader is drawn into the movement of being on the run he will spontaneously begin to feel as if he himself were on the run. Since the purpose of the writer is to involve the reader, to give him an experience of his own rather than instruct him, he is content to leave unsaid the most important element of all. Whatever the exact explanation, the absence of descriptions of inner apprehension is a paradoxical fact of thriller writing.

To be on the run first of all means to lose contact with whatever has made one secure. Second, it means having nowhere to turn. The first attribute of a settled society is that its inhabitants do not have firsthand experiences of this. This is the force behind Marmeladov's plaint in *Crime and Punishment*: " 'Do you understand what it means when you have absolutely nowhere to turn?' "[24] His perspective was destitution, and the man to whom he was speaking, Raskolnikov, would soon cut himself off from other men by a gratuitous murder. Arthur Rowe also had cut himself off by a mercy-killing. In all thrillers the hero, whose task it is to protect civilization, must first lose the protection of society. The hunter becomes the hunted. He needs friends. He will be lucky if he finds someone else like himself. "It was a gesture Leamas liked: it indicated that Peters, like himself, had been on the run."[25] The extreme suffering of loneliness, as many elderly persons experience it in nursing homes, is the place where no external recognition guarantees one's own sense of identity. To see someone else like oneself, even an enemy, is to be sure of oneself again. At times the loneliness is so demoralizing that the man on the run would almost prefer to be caught. "Sometimes he was like a man in flight, but running towards the enemy, desperate to feel upon his vanishing body the blows that would prove his being; desperate to imprint upon his sad conformity the mark of real purpose, desperate perhaps to abdicate his conscience in order to discover God."[26]

Unless the agent is caught or his cover is blown, he will usually be given the inner strength to pursue his lonely destiny. And it is very lonely. Loneliness is "the last law on earth," "the freezing point." Then why call it law? Because loneliness demands a rule of life, some sort of control, not only to bar panic and collapse, but to rope off the reasons for the loneliness and the hope of ultimate success and release. Any law needs a society to support and test it. Even the professional agent cannot live by himself forever. " '[They] have to live without sympathy . . . that's impossible, of course. [They] act it to one another, all this hardness; but [they] aren't like that really. I mean . . . one can't be out in the cold all the time; one has to come in from the cold.' "[27] And yet when the agent is engaged he is told, " 'If you do well you'll get no thanks and if you get into trouble you'll get no help.' "[28] But long before the end is reached, success or failure, loneliness and isolation must be endured. It is all the harder when one sees around one people going about their business normally. "The whole earth seemed full of laughter and happy movement. And it was shut off from me. I seemed to be living on the other side of a veil from this cheerful world."[29]

Terror

If the experience of being on the run were only the experience of being an exile, it would be bad enough. Exile is a state of mind as well as geographical displacement. Not to belong, not to have a home, can have long-term demoralizing effects, a permanent sickness undermining the basic confidences. That is not, however, the experience of being hunted. To vanish out of sight, and at the same time to be surrounded by condemnation rather than by acceptance, isolates one completely. In that isolation where no friendly word is spoken, the moral silence enclosing the self spawns unclothed terror.

Terror is not the same as fear. It is acknowledgment of a specific threat, unlike dread, which acknowledges the nameless. It is as intense as horror and like horror it cannot be sustained for long; unlike horror, however, it is pure anxiety, unmixed with loathing. "Fear's keen knife may cut and cut insatiably; it is a delicate torture at its most refined . . . horror may recur but it cannot be sustained; it dulls the senses."[30] Terror is uncontrolled fear which momentarily at least drives out all other awareness of reality. Its demands are insistent, rising in crescendo, until nerves can stand no more. One of the curious phenomena of city life is the plethora of horror films in poverty areas. Just as horror dulls the senses, so terror heightens them. The thriller reader looks for the latter rather than the former. Nothing contributes to this heightening of tension more precisely than the feeling of being stalked or being watched, the sense of ever-growing and ever-approaching danger. Dostoevsky is a master of this kind of suspense. " 'You know the feeling that someone is watching you, a sort of sensation which the mind receives without actual evidence.' "[31] Again and again Raskolnikov in *Crime and Punishment* and Prince Myshkin in *The Idiot* feel that they are being followed. "The prince became aware of two strange, burning eyes staring at him from among the crowd of people."[32] In his case, the strain became so unbearable that the raising of the murderer's knife over his heart coincided with an epileptic fit. There is always a limit which is never quite reached in fiction.

Danger

To be on the run has a momentum of its own. No one has understood this better than Max Picard. "Whithersoever they may flee, there is God."[33] Take out the word "God" and substitute some enemy's name, and Picard's acceleration can be felt: "Wherever they find themselves, once more they flee away, for God is everywhere. Ever more desperately they flee; but God is already in every place, waiting for them to come. There is no place where God cannot be, therefore there is no place from which the Flight is absent. The Flight is great, for God is great."[34] The hunted hero is not just a victim, he is one who "couldn't resist the temptation to stalk the impossible."[35] As a result he has to develop "the reasoning of a hunted beast"[36] if he wants to survive. Some mistakes might be avoided if the agent is properly trained; but every situation is different, and things happen so fast that instinct is just as important as training.

Apart from training, the difference between the amateur and professional agent is that the latter will have to stay out in the cold again and again, in hiding, on the run. He can look forward to some repetition of a life which is radically abnormal. Each time, the changeover is heralded and initiated by the presence of and his awareness of danger. Without danger there would be no new experience, no descent into hell. To most of us danger is remote and abstract, something that can happen but probably will not, something that happens to others. In that sense, danger is usually a misnomer for possible evil, or evil once-removed. When evil takes an interest in us, and moves our way, then we speak of danger. " 'They'll try to get you in the dark.' This was danger: this suspense was what somebody else had experienced."[37] Danger is the approach of evil from some other world to our own. The supposition is that one moment our world is free of danger and secure, and the next moment filled with danger and empty of all other concerns.

When in danger, it is possible—for some people for the first time in their lives—to sympathize with others. There is a fellowship of danger just as there is a ministry of fear. That fellowship holds its members in suspense. Not only are they withdrawn from their former preoccupations and companions, each is aware that his personal fate is now on

the line. Suspense involves more than waiting; not all waiting is suspenseful. For suspense means tension plus uncertainty, and danger above all other causes produces that.
Too much suspense or tension can be as harmful as the
shadow of evil behind the danger. It can erode the spirit until it is anesthetized against the very evil that it has feared.
" 'One of the things which danger does to you after a time
is to kill emotion. I don't think I shall ever feel anything
again except fear. None of us can hate anymore—or
love.' "[38] Indeed, there is no emotion, not even fear, that
cannot be killed by excessive suspense. Who can tell ahead
of time whether "unbearable suspense" will dull sensitivity
to reality or set off an explosion? That also happens, and is
usually regarded as the greater danger. At what point will
a man break? For some men and women suspense is harder
to bear than torture; for them it is the supreme torture. To
bear suspense requires a different kind of self-control, a
different kind of waiting.

Tension

On the other hand, for some people conspiracy is a way
of life. "Darsoss wondered if he could live without the
constant presence of conspiracy, without hatred, without
tension from minute to minute."[39] We all know people who
treat everything that happens or might happen as if it were
a conspiracy or a tragedy. We do not believe them, and
their insistence gets on our nerves. We know it is not good
to live in perpetual suspense or in the shadow of evil. It is
also difficult to believe that others can really think that life
is a conspiracy with so much evidence of security surround-
ing them. Rather do we say of them that they are neuroti-

cally obsessed. And yet we should be able to recognize the damage that is done to some emotional types by suffering or threat of pain, and we should distinguish this loss of perspective from the egotism that wants to be in the center of reality, an imaginary reality. On the other hand, once tension takes hold of anyone, it is difficult to be released from it, and when the release does come, it can come as a letdown, which is as harmful to the nervous system as the sudden introduction of danger. For some few, danger and tension become a way of life with positive values. The concentration of evil forces a man to decide what is of absolute importance and to find the means within himself to safeguard it. It is hard for some to return to a social climate in which good and evil are ungraded, and one thing is about as important as another.

From the point of view of a thriller reader, who of course is in no danger of anything except boredom, his reading can induce a kind of tension, but pleasurable instead of insupportable. There is pleasure to be experienced in following the developing confrontation between the heroic and the demonic. Thriller readers can find their release from the tensions of their own lives by transferring their concern to the tensions of fictional reality. They experience a merging of their normal tensions within the unusual tensions of fiction. When in the course of a novel the tension is broken by success, their own tensions, now forgotten, will have been eased. This therapy can be undertaken again and again, until the overcomplexity or insipidity or repetitiousness of plot and characterization fails to evoke a sufficient sense of reality.

Not all reasons for reading thrillers are obvious. Even though it may be true that "there is a large reservoir of anger and hatred in all of us,"[40] it would be unfair to assume that we all read thrillers to let loose our rages harmlessly. Probably few do. Many more discover that they can respond sympathetically to malevolence and victimization because they have experienced moral ambivalence firsthand. Both Graham Greene and John Le Carré possess the extraordinary power, especially among thriller writers, of being able to force the reader into self-examination and self-judgment. Through them we see our own self-deceptions and nostalgias.

Better that than to come to the place of absolute failure. " 'It's a failure people don't get over,' "[41] says Greene, ". . . the freezing point of knowing absolute failure."[42] Among other things, this too is an apprehension that the reader brings to his reading of the thriller. For not only does he want to admire the success of someone with whom he makes an effort to identify himself, he welcomes the description of any tension. Tension at least represents life going on, unfinished. When we are reminded of failure, we hope to be told that collapse is not the only alternative. We should meet failure, vicariously if not in real life, "as one day [we] would probably meet death, with cynical resentment and the courage of a solitary."[43]

Chaos

All thrillers are basically concerned about two things: death and responsibility. Tillich may have been right in thinking that the anxiety of meaninglessness is the characteristic anxiety of our time. The popularity of the "death of God" debate seemed to confirm this. Few of us talk about personal death or guilt, or seem much concerned about either. But we read about them in thriller literature. What we do not acknowledge openly and directly, we at least read about. The thriller world is Heideggerian rather than Tillichian. Its categories do not include meaninglessness, but rather Care, Dread, Death, Guilt, Time, and a Being-unto-Death, all the categories of contingency and resolution that we find in even the run-of-the-mill detective or spy story. If the categories of danger, tension, death, heroism are Heidegger's, the mood and momentum are Dostoevsky's. The atmosphere of the thriller is feverish, with that airless, suffocating tenseness of the gambling table or the guilt-ridden soul. Desperate and harsh, the destiny of man must be decided at any second. Desperate and alive, for once you were dead "what did it matter where you lay . . . in a dirty sump or in a marble tower on top of a high hill? You were dead, you were sleeping the big sleep."[44] The reader agrees that it is better to live dangerously than not to have lived at all, better even to read a poorly written and shallow thriller once in a while than to forget what life is for others right now.

The Unexpected

John Buchan was the first thriller writer to put into words this essential difference between a thriller and any other kind of fiction. "Now I saw how thin is the protection of civilization. An accident and a bogus ambulance—a false charge and a bogus arrest—there were a dozen ways of spiriting one out of this gay and bustling world."[45] Civilization means at least two quite different things: protection from chaos on the one hand and the development of the "phenomenon of man" on the other. It is the first of these that is in jeopardy in the thriller, and so easily removed by accidental encounter with the enemies of civilization burrowing within. The reader is well aware that the thin protection is removed every day from countless people; he is told by TV and newspapers of only some of them.

Nor does the reader need to be scared so that he can thank God that he himself is still safe, or so that his sympathies with the unprotected can be deepened. No, a reader wants to see for himself, and feel for himself—vicariously and safely, of course—what life looks like in the middle of chaos. We do not need to go so far as to claim that everyone has a secret instinct for chaos, as Dostoevsky said: " 'They all say they hate evil, but in their heart of hearts they all love it.' "[46] It is enough to recognize that many do love evil to one degree or another, and some let it ride free in their dreams and fantasies, and in their leisure reading.

Apart from a taste for sadism, some of us welcome the chance to imagine what it would be like if we were really on our own, without home and friends and legal recourse, and were put to the test of having not only to fend for ourselves, like Robinson Crusoe, but to hide from intelligent savages who knew where we were and were closing in on us. This is what Rose Cullen does not want to take in, when D tells her he has just been shot at on a London street. " 'Don't you see that if things like that happened, life would be quite different. One would have to begin over again.' "[47] That is just it, one's point of view on life would have to be completely altered. Although we may doubt that most thriller readers are prepared to have that happen to them, they are fascinated with the transformation as they see it taking place in someone else. As a prospective victim, the hero arouses both sympathy and relief that we are not in his shoes. And because we have been encouraged by the author to like this person, we would be pleased to see him succeed against all odds—the greater the odds the more we will admire him, and ourselves indirectly for liking him. But before our sense of virtue is flattered blind, we should not forget that the thrill in the thriller comes not so much from the hero's success as from those moments of fear and tension before he has won through. In these moments the reader feels that this is what it must be to be really alive.

Just so do people recall their own times of personal crisis, war, accidents, death in the family, being in love. Then they were really alive, and life has not been that real, or that painful, ever since. Some were taught to value life more, to care for others more, to be grateful and glad for small favors and unexpected beauty. Some were taught also to honor courage and endurance, honesty and friendship. They recall that crisis was their profoundest teacher. Especially in a century when civilization, so massive and so secure, seems so perfectly equipped to protect all, two world wars and satellite conflicts have brought home to millions not only the truth of Buchan's insight, but a fact that Greene expressed through a dream of Arthur Rowe: " 'Thrillers are like life—more like life than you are . . . it's what we've all made of the world.' "[48] In this dream he is speaking to his mother, now dead, and tells her that real life is not " 'tea on the lawn, evensong, croquet,' " but such situations as he finds himself now in: " 'I'm wanted for a murder I didn't do. People want to kill me because I know too much. I'm hiding underground . . .' "[49] The point of this passage is the main element in any thriller, a sudden reversal of expectation. That this reversal takes place so often in the twentieth century still has not caused us to change our expectations.

We are disturbed by reversals because we feel that it should not be like this—we are still civilized and therefore still surrounded by barriers and by legal help, if not friends. And yet, out of the blue catastrophe pours.

For the thriller reader catastrophe rains when we are happy as well as when we are bored. It would be a mistake to assume that only bored men and women read thrillers. In the thrillers themselves the crack in civilization may open when the hero is blissfully content (Richard Hannay at the beginning of *The Three Hostages*) or when he is fed up with life (Hannay at the beginning of *The Thirty-Nine Steps*). The crack can appear at any time, any place, and to any person, but naturally in fiction mainly to the brave. Another word for this crack is the unexpected. Ambler's solemn remark in *The Mask of Dimitrios* about chance, "Chance plays an important if not predominant part in human affairs,"[50] is an understatement when applied to the thriller. There could be no thriller without chance. No matter how calculating the powers of evil are, it is only by chance that this man or that finds himself in their way. Even when the hero is himself a professional, it is chance that he rather than someone else in his service should have this particular adventure. Writers retain their ability to shock the reader by introducing the fortuitous and unforeseen. The earlier thrillers' use of civilians and amateurs only makes it easier to demonstrate the plausibility of the crisis which arises out of an unlooked-for meeting of opposites. Even chance has to be made plausible for the reader. He must be able to feel, "This could be me. There but for the grace of real life go I."

Identity Crisis

The unexpected has a role to play in fiction in general, but in the thriller it plays the lead. In this category a world is packaged. For comparison we might remind ourselves of Stendhal's use of this in *The Red and the Black*. Julien Sorel is either craving the unexpected or being repelled by the horror of the unexpected on the part of most of the people he meets. They like things the way they are; he is inordinately ambitious, desiring power and position. Above all, he dreams of being a great lover. Out of the most innocent and proper opportunities he calculates to squeeze every advantage for himself. He ascends quickly toward his goals without scruple and yet with a soft heart. For him life is not like a conspiracy, it is a conspiracy. He calculates so self-consciously that he wears out his capacity to savor unforeseen success when it actually comes his way. In the end his fall is more rapid than his rise, and equally unexpected. He has brought about the fall by his inability to cope with an unexpected threat, from someone he loves, to the position he has made for himself. If this novel proves many things, one thing above all it does show, that the unexpected cannot be controlled, not by courage or intelligence, not by innocence or sophistication. It has its own rules, and no one has yet discovered them.

Stendhal also understood that without the *"imprévu"* there is no charm in human existence. Nothing was more characteristic than the delight he took, as a man and as a writer, in dreaming of the joys of meeting a beautiful woman who would love him, or gazing out over a beautiful landscape, or abandoning himself to beautiful music. His writing recaptures such moments for us in such a way that we recall our own past and believe in our own nostalgia for what is still to come. Novelty rather than shock, delight rather than bewilderment, these are authentic responses to the unexpected. But so are terror and pain. We find the latter in the thriller, where the unexpected is not beautiful and charming. On the contrary, by chance one man—and maybe more—is withdrawn abruptly from all he is used to and is set, as in a nightmare, in the middle of a strange stage where none of the rules he has lived by are observed or can be used. The unexpected commits him and his destiny to an order of things which can be properly called conspiratorial, and where he must learn new and perhaps despised rules in order to survive. Le Carré's Leclerc, pathetic and despicable parody of an intelligence officer, reminds his gullible subordinate that " 'It's easy to forget what intelligence consists of: luck and speculation.' "[51] Ironically, he is speaking the truth, for without luck speculation is useless, and Leclerc has no luck. Even bumblers can be saved with a little bit of luck. Saved, not crowned; for to win requires more than luck and speculation, it requires action.

A man is to be defined by his deeds rather than by his security. Each thriller tells the story of some man's achievement of his identity on a battlefield bounded by chance and control. Interrogation alone will not win this war, nor does discovery take the place of achievement. There can be no resting place until the battle is won or the enemy eluded. What figures as an identity crisis for the hero is in a way an identity crisis for the reader too. He is reading about man in crisis because he has not yet worked out to his satisfaction his own identity. Vicarious experience gives him a dry run and enables him to come to sharper terms with his own dissatisfactions.

Deception and Mistrust

The way of achievement, for the reader as for the hero, is by no means sharp at the outset, except as the shock of crisis is sharp. The sudden transfer from a secure world to an insecure world does not take place without losing one's bearings. In addition, after the initial encounter, the enemy's true character is not menace but deception. The heart of evil is deception, a power of lies. This is Dashiell Hammett's contribution, and it is absolutely fundamental. Violence and the threat of violence are always in the background if not the foreground of the thriller, as they are in the real world. Even violence is not absolutely basic; it is but the explosive result of the tension generated by deception. In Hammett's novels the detective's relentless quest and inquisition sooner or later force deceivers to founder on their own lies; an explosion occurs, and then there is peace. Ned Beaumont and Sam Spade are the catalytic agents of this process; they press the crossed wires of lies tighter and tighter until the charge they carry is too burning for them to bear, and the subsequent flash melts them down. The hero himself is left limp and empty; there is no joy, not even satisfaction.

Evil cannot afford to speak the truth; more than that, it cannot afford to reveal itself as it really is, something to be understood only in terms of its opposite, the real. It is nothing in itself, and because of that it diminishes or annihilates anything it touches, subtracts from being. This is the worst pain of all, withdrawal. The detective or the spy must find out who is the biggest liar, the biggest nothing, and then he will uncover Satan, the spider in the middle of the conspiratorial web. Following the clues that lead through the labyrinth requires patience, intelligence, and luck, and the greatest risk is that the constant necessity of discounting someone else's deceptions will dim one's own sense of identity and value. The agent can be corrupted—Chandler's books are full of bad cops—by his own profession. " 'They're cheats,' he broke out suddenly. 'That's an odd word, I know, to use about a sister service, John. Lying's second nature to them. Half of them don't know any longer when they're telling the truth.' "[52] And yet this danger is small compared with the perennially unstable, the demoniacal villains who, having nothing real and good to believe in, in the end cannot keep track of their own lies and become entangled in their own deceits. If the detective or spy is patient, he will be rewarded by seeing this happen. Brigid O'Shaughnessy in *The Maltese Falcon* cries, " 'Oh, I'm so tired, tired of it all, of myself, of lying and thinking up lies, and of not knowing what is a lie and what is the truth.' "[53] The fatigue of constant deception, exhausting one's tiny grain of identity to keep from making a slip, can hardly be endured forever. Perhaps this is why mankind has kept on feeling that evil is self-destructive. This is what Graham Greene means when he speaks of someone entering "the territory of lies without a passport for return."[54] The agent's "profession was to lie, to have the quick story ready."[55] Similarly for the lover who, in deceiving his wife, would finally feel "tired by all the lies he would sometime have to tell"[56] and "haunted by the vision of an endless distrust."[57]

The meaning of chaos is just this, that in it you no longer know where you are, who you are, and who anybody else is. " 'You can't trust anyone.' "[58] "He knew he could trust himself. He knew nothing else. . . . There was no trust anywhere."[59] In the end it is an illusion to suppose that you can trust yourself either. This is what Gabriel Marcel is talking about when he says that "we live in a world where betrayal is possible at every moment and in every form."[60] No one can be completely depended on. Is this true? As true as the confidence one has in a friend or relative ("I can always count on him")? Always? For what? To what extent? We get dizzy thinking about the claims and counterclaims. We feel the dizziness, and perhaps the nausea, of chaos. When "treachery darkens the whole world,"[61] we cease to be a "being-in-the-world,"[62] and become a cipher known by a cover or a code number, as easily assignable to our enemy or comrade as to ourselves. This is the real identity crisis, at the heart of the chaos of cover, lies, deception, and betrayal.

Greene makes an interesting suggestion when he says that "it is impossible to go through life without trust; that is to be imprisoned in the worst cell of all, oneself."[63] He is probably right in thinking that it is impossible, and maybe he should have said "hell" instead of "cell." But, without trust, is there after a while any self at all to retreat to? Or is the emptiness now so yawning that it is only the ghost of a vanished identity? Just before the self fades from sight, the last stage is reached when it can no longer figure out how or why anything has happened, and no longer cares. "He [Smiley] reflected for the hundredth time on the obscurity of motive in human action; there is no true thing on earth. There is no constant, no dependable point, not even in the purest logic or the most obscure mysticism; least of all in the motives of men when they are moved to act violently."[64] We might say that there is a progression in a crisis from a chance encounter to reversal of position (from security to danger), to the tension of resolution, to deception, to confusion, to fatigue, to emptiness. Or so it would go if the hero failed; this is the specter which consciously or not evokes the thrill in the reader and the challenge to the hero.

Violence

The challenge would fade if not accepted, and the thrill would pass. For the hero is not challenged to enter chaos and be swamped, nor does the reader wish to contemplate emptiness. Both hero and reader stand before that which above all must be avoided, and their excitement is caused in part by their dread that it may not be avoided, and in part by their expectation of a way out. If the way out were only a matter of taking certain prescribed steps in a more or less prescribed order, there would be no excitement at all, except in whatever magnetic attraction the void itself might exercise. The expectation of the thriller reader by this time extends, sometimes secretly but more often now openly, far beyond the conventional bounds of security and propriety to an alternative that reflects chaos itself.

Violence matches chaos; it belongs, as it were, to the same philosophical family. It reflects it as a spark is struck off metal. If violence is an answer to chaos, it is not because it negates it, but rather because it is suggested by it. The vertigo experienced by the hero as he looks into the vortex of danger, betrayal, and the kaleidoscope of motive and meaning cannot be borne for long. (Every man's tolerance has a limit, where he loses touch with reality.) Paralysis means capture as well as loss of confidence and identity. Whether we call the recognition of the ultimate menace of chaos vertigo, or whether we call it tension, there is always a point and time reached, for however short a time, when we know we have three alternatives: to yield, to get out, or to explode. Violence is the third option. Sometimes violence opens the door to the second option, salvation. But quite as often, it is ineffective and only confirms chaos. Release can be purchased at the price of absolute defeat.

It has been said often enough that violence is the manner and sign of our time. Perhaps violence is no more the core of our time than chaos, or chaos than structure and order. Perhaps we only understand violence better now (if so, why now?). Violence is always a temptation for a frustrated man or nation, and there are many kinds of frustration in our century. When someone knows what he wants and cannot accept that it is not for him, violence becomes an alternative to working and waiting. A large part of mankind now thinks it does know what it should have, and is becoming increasingly unwilling to accept deferment or refusal. The second alternative, which logically should be the last resort, is all too often the impatient, angry, first and only resort. In this sense, violence is a clue to our time. It cannot be understood by itself, particularly apart from the dream of completeness and fulfillment that precedes frustration and violence, both in logic and in fact.

Every thriller expresses, directly or indirectly, some dream of human completeness and fulfillment. This is the romantic element without which the thriller would be only a record of disintegration. The exhibition of heroism amid adversity is usually concluded by some act of poetic justice. The thriller at its best is a compound of romance and an excursion into and out of chaos. When the romantic or heroic element is missing or neglected, when all the characters are corrupt or shoddy, the reader goes away with a bad taste in his mouth and the conviction that he has been let down. He has been lured on to read by the prospect of a strip-show of the worst in man, only to discover that the worst in man without something of the best is disgusting or just boring. There is formula-writing, for the sake of making money, which uses only part of the formula, and it appeals only to the man who has lost his integrity and no longer cares. Sometimes we find ourselves saying, "But these characters are not human, not worth bothering with. They have no ideals, no fidelities, no commitments, no love, only reactions and sensations. They do not even carry about with them a meaningful environment." Greene, in his review of Buchan, had observed this too: "What is remarkable about these adventure-stories is the completeness of the world they describe. The backgrounds to many of us may not be sympathetic, but they are elaborately worked in: each character carries round with him his school, his regiment, his religious beliefs, often touched with Calvinism: memories of grouse-shooting and deer-stalking, of sport at Eton, debates in the House."[65] Greene's own characters are always complete, and we have only to think of James Bond in this connection to realize just how empty a "hero" can be, and then to wonder about our own motives for liking him. For some of us he only comes alive when he is being beaten up.

Is this true of some readers as well, that they too come alive only in their attraction to violence? Perhaps the question will be clearer, and easier to answer, as soon as we add sex to violence. The taste for one is no longer satisfied unless the taste for the other is satisfied too. As I have noted earlier, Buchan did not feel he needed either sex or violence, and although the threat of violence is always implied, it is not spelled out, and sex is not even hinted at. In the case of

Household (writing in the shadow of Buchan), violence, including torture, is explicit, and sex is only hinted at. Ambler at least began as a sexless writer, although all his books dealt with violence as explicitly as Chandler or Fleming. In real life the two are connected. Violence, as the controlled or uncontrolled transgressing of the bounds of force required to accomplish an end, might even be called rape. For this is really what we are dealing with in the thriller when we say "sex." It is not the ultimate physical expression of the love of two persons, but the violent release of one person's tension by means of the other. In the thriller sex is rape, actual or disguised, and appears for the same reason as violence, to bring about release from an emotional impasse. "There was something enigmatic about her which was a constant stimulus . . . and now he knew that she was profoundly, excitingly sensual, but that the conquest of her body, because of the central privacy in her, would each time have the tang of rape."[66] In Chandler and Fleming the hero is sometimes rewarded by sex after his trials are over. Or would it be more accurate to say that if there is any residue of tension after he has achieved victory over the forces of chaos, a harmless but violent emptying of himself into someone who is passive and neutral will allay it?

In this regard it is instructive to compare briefly the revulsion felt by Greene's heroes, and the amoral acceptance of violence by James Bond. The code name "007" means Bond has a license to kill, and the reader hopes he will. Both Arthur Rowe and D are men averse to violence. They "stood on the frontier of violence, a strange land [they] had never visited before,"[67] but they did not like standing there. Violence is infectious, as Greene remarked, and becomes a way of life. Neither Rowe nor D was corrupt, even though they carried the infection in them. "Violence went with them everywhere."[68] It is appropriate that their relations with women were romantic rather than sensual. This is true of the early and best Chandler. It is only when Marlowe becomes emotionally spent that he is willing to go to bed with anyone. He may never have been Galahad; at the end he is not even Launcelot.

It is too bad that violence and sex should be equated at all, for there is nothing good to say about violence. Sex is more ambiguous, as we all know. When it is an expression of fulfillment of metaphysical longing, nothing is as desirable. But this kind of hunger is curiously absent from most thrillers, in spite of a certain romantic strain in the early thriller. The reason seems to be that just as too much violence can blunt all our emotions, too much danger discourages the development, at least temporarily, of this most exemplary interpersonal relationship. Love—and sex in love —has conditions of its own: time, privacy, exclusive concentration. It cannot easily survive distractions. Nothing is more distracting than danger and violence. That is why what might otherwise have been part of the course of fulfillment of a person, is converted into a release from tension.

One often hears it said that a love of violence is symbolic of man's wish to rebel against social constraints and repression. This is probably true enough for those people who feel so shackled. Not everyone does, and even some who are frustrated really do not wish to be released through the gate of violence. To some it may be inconceivable that others prefer another way, the way of reason and patience, love and fulfillment. Violence is not that attractive, particularly to those who have experienced its results. Besides, for the man, call him hero, who carries with him into chaos, real or imaginary, the dream of justice and love, nothing is ever solved by violence and rape. Even readers of thrillers sometimes know the difference and object to having one kind of hero and solution palmed off on them instead of being allowed to identify themselves with someone with integrity and intelligence. On the other hand, it may be that, even if the thriller does not appeal directly to secret desires to break loose and violate, it may appeal to something more subtle, namely, an underdeveloped or thwarted longing for fulfillment. In the end, the thriller, each novel, must be rated according to whether its heroes stand firm in the middle of chaos, or whether they are converted by chaos and are damned.

·◦❴3❵◦·

THE READER:
His Inner World

The Emotions

If plots of thrillers bear any resemblance to the methods of actual intelligence operations it is purely coincidental. No one who is professionally familiar with a security or espionage organization should expect to find in books written by men who have never been agents, representations of counterintelligence as it is actually practiced. It is unfortunate that so many writers give us the impression that they would like to be thought of as retired intelligence officers. Perhaps some readers look for this. But any attempt to impress readers by smothering them with complex procedural material can end by boring them. The nature and purpose of the thriller is then changed into something else.

Thrillers are not meant to be documentaries, or even fictional accounts of the lives of real spies. They are not concerned with the real or external world at all. Rather, they are written for the sake of and written about the interior life of man. Of course, the categories of the thriller are categories of experience, but reality as experienced by the human subject, as appearing to and inside the human subject. This is a self-contained world, with its own categories and an appropriate symbolism (i.e., a plot), an objective correlative. In real life, that is, when one is not reading thrillers, we are tuned up by chance and by crises. Chance or crisis, however, is not assimilated easily, sometimes not at all. If they were, we would not need to brood on, dream of, and re-present in appropriate symbols their impact and challenge. We wish to record the crisis and the unresolved or unresolvable tension so that we may better live with it or understand it. One way, and only one way, to do so is to create neutral, impersonal, but also typical symbols for the nature of our experience. In the thriller the symbol that identifies the experience of personal crisis and tension is that of being on the run. The imagination then adds to this the other elements of such an experience that are suggested by its own appropriate logic. The reader does not need to have had a similar experience in order to identify himself with this artificial symbol. He accepts the rules of the game in order to immerse his own feelings in the similar feelings of the man in the fictional situation. In fact, he may well find himself being amused at the spectacle of being able to identify himself with someone in a situation he could not possibly expect ever to be in or would want to be in. His amusement would not by any means lessen his more serious sympathy with the plight of the hero.

The thriller is therefore always therapeutic, for writer as well as reader. It is not only a work of the imagination, and not of the scientific mind, it reveals the inner world of motives, desires, and conflicts, using representations of the outer world only as a means to draw the motives, desires, and conflicts out into the open. The main question raised by the thriller is not what kind of world we live in, or what reality is like, but what it has done to us. The thriller is not by any means oriented outward toward the shape of the world, but inward to the heart of the subject. We go along with arbitrary, stock situations and plots for the sake of something far more real, pressing, and serious, namely, the character of our inner life. When, as sometimes happens, these stock situations and characters are repeated in fact, we should not make the mistake of thinking that now at last we are reading about the truth. Fiction and romance do not need facts to tell the truth, unless by facts we mean the shape of our emotional life.

Thomas Narcejac's very perceptive little book (unfortunately out of print and not available even in major university libraries), *La Fin d'un Bluff*, is one of the rare attempts to discuss this. He maintains that the detective story and the spy story are to be distinguished by their quite different attitudes toward the universe, the first falling back on a closed universe and the second assuming an open one. It is easy enough to see the acuity of this. In detective stories, crime only threatens to destroy or upset a portion of society, whereas in the spy story civilization itself is undermined. Further, the detective assumes, correctly, that all he has to do is to employ his reason carefully and the mystery will be solved. The hero of a spy story—unless it is just a detective story in different dress—is forced to function in a different kind of world, where reason alone cannot win the victory, and where the mystery itself is not the problem or conflict that must be resolved, but rather the emotional effects which that conflict has on the hero and on the reader. The detective story sets forth a problem to be solved; the spy story sets forth an adventure of the spirit. "The thriller obliges the reader to admit provisionally that the absurd is perhaps possible. And this simple thought engenders a profound and delightful anguish, made of fear and credulity (for the inexplicable resembles the supernatural), but also of security and pleasure (for reason triumphs over problems which seem insoluble)."[1]

The reader has always known that the absurd is possible, in general, but not necessarily for him. The thriller is written to appeal directly to the reader's desires even more than his memories. We can believe in chance and crisis because we have experienced both, but usually we are not given a chance to function heroically in a crisis, but only to endure. The absurd that evokes both anguish and delight is an absurd that threatens to be overwhelming and yet one that we are encouraged and commissioned to face. Narcejac is wrong, however, in suggesting that "reason triumphs over problems which seem insoluble." Man may triumph, but not by reason alone. That is the difference between the detective and the hero of the adventure story. The latter succeeds (and in certain circumstances endurance is success by other, more personal qualities: moral vision, courage, fidelity, and the willingness to put himself on the line.

Boredom

Whatever the mode and manner of heroism, the thriller reader not only admits that the absurd is possible, he ardently desires the absurd, and not only because it will give him the unwonted opportunity to shine, but because it will shake him out of the lethargic expectation of security and more security. Even when boredom is not a fact prior to reading, it is always lounging just off stage. Both Buchan and Fleming have openly used boredom as a springboard for adventure. "It was one of those days when it seemed to James Bond that all life, as someone put it, was nothing but

a heap of six to four against."[2] With no dangerous assignments, and nothing to do except sit around an office and do
paper work, 007 becomes so dull to himself and out of sorts
with everyone else that M. sends him to Shrublands for a
cure. There he meets a Count Lippe, an agent of Spectre.
They get on each other's nerves immediately. And so the
Count manages to stretch James' spine on a spine-stretch-
ing machine (once called the rack) and James, in turn, manages to toast the Count to a crisp in a Turkish bath. "The
outcome of this rather childish trial of strength between
two extremely tough and ruthless men, in the bizarre sur-
roundings of a nature clinic in Sussex, was to upset, if only
in a minute fashion, the exactly timed machinery of a plot
that was about to shake the governments of the Western
world."[3] A lively, plausible (because the emotional logic is
right), and childish beginning to an otherwise inferior
Fleming.

In an earlier book he had spelled out the problem of boredom even more plainly:

The blubbery arms of the soft life had Bond round the neck
and they were slowly strangling him. He was a man of war
and when, for a long period, there was no war, his spirit
went into a decline. . . . [He] awoke . . . and was disgusted
to find that he was thoroughly bored with the prospect of
the day ahead. Just as, in at least one religion, *accidie* is the
first of the cardinal sins, so boredom . . . was the only vice
Bond utterly condemned.[4]

I do not know which religion (or which Christian brand of
asceticism, if that is what Fleming meant) holds accidie to
be the first of the cardinal sins. I do wonder whether, apart
from this passage recording Fleming's own struggle with
accidie, it also appeals to the reader's willingness to think

of himself as a warrior in temporary decline rather than as the dullard he really is. This is a good example of the emotional logic of thrillers, where emotional changes within the story correspond to a wished-for change within the reader.

John Buchan not only began the first of his thrillers with Hannay's boredom; ten years later, in *John McNab*, he devoted an entire story to the efforts of three eminent and successful men to conquer acedia and recover their usual zest for living. Bored with their work, their success, their comforts, and pleasures, they took the advice of a doctor friend who said, " 'You've got to rediscover the comforts of your life by losing them for a little.' "[5] They went poaching in Scotland. Like Bond they were bored, but they, being better read than 007 (Buchan being better read than Fleming), knew exactly what they suffered from: " 'It's what the Middle Ages suffered from—and it's called *taedium vitae*. It's a special kind of ennui.' "[6] The worst kind. The physician's prescription is, of course, the same prescription silently offered by each paperback, rediscovering life by losing it for a little. The only difference is that the reader has to pretend by involving himself—as the reader of a detective story seldom does—in the emotional course of the story. When the three gentlemen poachers in *John McNab* reveal their true identities, they are assured that they were never in danger of being exposed by the landlord on whose estate they were captured, for to do so would " 'weaken the public prestige of a statesman I believe in, a great lawyer I brief, and a great banker whose assistance is of the utmost value to me.' "[7] These three men were buttresses of "the solid structure of society,"[8] and it is inconceivable that anyone believing in that structure would carelessly condemn or ridicule them, except predictably irresponsible journalists. Buchan seems to have had no conception of the special pleasure many people take in seeing or believing the worst about the best. At times Buchan was curiously unworldly. He could go only so far as to understand the final irony of all artificial attempts to break loose. " 'We thought we had got outside civilization and were really taking chances. But we weren't.' "[9] This is just as true of readers and their vicarious adventures of the spirit as of the characters they read about. In the end they are back with themselves. They have taken a trip, like dope addicts, but unlike the latter they had become alienated not from society but from themselves. The thriller does not provide final therapy.

Escape

What it does offer is escape. Of course, so do drinking, drug-taking, and madness. Ambler tells the story of a man who could not stand Central Europe in the middle of our century, and who went mad as a refuge from it: " 'It hurt him too much to stay sane in a crazy world. He had to find a way of escape, to make his own world, a world in which he counted. His mind created the lie for him, and now he is happy. He's escaped from everybody's insanity into his own private one.' "[10] There are many like him, in and out of institutions. It need not be insanity that one wants to escape from, but more mundane things such as lack of privacy, too much pressure and tension, too much acceleration, and too many things to keep in mind. It is not grotesque evil, cruelty, mass destruction that upset most people, but noise and insecurity, snubs and failure.

This is why Julian Symons' prerequisite for enjoyment

cannot be accepted at face value: "A high degree of personal security is necessary to the full enjoyment of the detective story."[11] Perhaps so, since we are so often reminded that it is the bedtime reading of bishops and statesmen. Would the problem be different if Symons had said "spy story" instead? Probably not. One does not have to try to escape anything in order to enjoy a thriller, except tension and pressure. The form the relief takes is not primarily neutral—release, distraction, tranquillity—but something positive and concretely imagined, namely, an adventure. When we read fiction we do not just leave our boredom or our cares; we also participate in the discovery of another world where for a time we can be transfigured. One might say that the essential purpose of the thriller is transfiguration.

This is why it is possible one minute to talk of the thriller as an escape, and the next minute as a fantasy. The fantasy is the escape. What is fantasy? A compound of the desirable and the preposterous in the form of a dream. We like our fantasies, or else we would not create them. We even want to dream the preposterous, whether grotesque or harmless, provided we give ourselves a chance to play hero. We want a world where for once we count, where "I alone can save." We know this is preposterous, and so we are willing to assume an environment for our heroism equally preposterous. Occasionally, something happens in real life, the improbable becomes incarnate. Then our rigid sense of the chasm between the probable and the improbable is shaken. This is not the way it is meant to be. We have now the choice of living up to the truth, or being defeated by it. We usually decide to accept it, and sometimes we are gratified to find out that fiction is earlier than fact, dream prior to reality. "I knew it was the passionate wish of his heart, somehow and somewhere to get a chance of turning his knowledge of this coast to practical account in the war that he felt was bound to come, to play that 'splendid game' in this, the most fascinating field for it."[12]

Davies, patriotic dreamer, got his chance to play the game, one which he, awkward and candid, should have been the last to have played well, the great game of espionage. Long before Childers' book, Kipling had written in *Kim* of "the great Game," played in India by Babus and boys against tribesmen and Russians. Even with the destiny of India at stake, "what he [Kim] loved was the game for its own sake,"[13] in one word, adventure. This is not like saying that the detective likes his work because he likes solving puzzles, and not because he feels responsible for the welfare of society. He will probably feel both, and still not by any means be classifiable as an adventurer. Nor will the reader of a detective story be prepared to tune in his emotions on those of any fictional person. When you read about an adventure, you go riding along yourself. When someone cooperates with fiction, instead of standing off from it, he apprehends the new experience under the ambivalent form of both plausible and implausible, the near and the remote.

Adventure

Georg Simmel's analysis of "adventure" is as relevant to our understanding of the thriller as he meant it to be to the life of the artist, the gambler, or the lover. He said that adventure is "dropping out of the continuity of life" while remaining "connected with the center."[14] Isn't this just what the spy does? When he assumes a false identity, or when he is on the run, he drops out of his own continuum, and that of the public at large. In one way or another, he has broken with his own past and the public's present. The question then arises, and the question is his crisis, is he completely disconnected? Or is he still, or even more, connected with himself? If so, then obviously not with the self everyone knows most about, but with some hidden or secret self. In what sense can this hidden self, unused, so far unseen, be called his center? That is a difficult question to answer, and for some the very question is embarrassing. Not everyone likes to admit that his fantasies, or his enjoyment of fantasies, are part of the definition of his personality. We are often ashamed to confess our fantasy life. Simmel says that "in the adventure . . . we forcibly pull the world into ourselves . . . [and] abandon ourselves to the world with fewer defenses and reserves."[15] But that is precisely where the trouble lies, in our abandonment, with fewer defenses and reserves. Civilization has come to mean, in large part, the building up of reserves. These protect us from both "the terror by night . . . [and] the arrow that flieth by day . . . the pestilence that walketh in darkness [and] . . . the sickness that destroyeth in the noon-day."[16]

The adventurer creates his own world, as does the reader who is an adventurer at heart. He makes use of what he finds, and gives it what he has. An adventure gives a man a chance to find out what he has got, who he really is at bottom. And so the hoary lines about "when the chips are down," "the men and the boys," etc. If life has dealt us bad cards, we will make up a new pack. In doing so we almost always become isolated. "When he comes to the Great Game, he must go alone," without security, help, recognition, and one's own reserves, and into a new land and new

climate, feverish and suffocating. Perhaps we should qual-
ify the last word. There can be an adventure, a certain stage
of adventure, sometimes called "high adventure," when,
as in a love affair, the mind apprehends the crisis exclusively as a challenge he feels ready for. Then the climate, far
from being suffocating, is exhilarating. Again as in a love
affair, so in espionage, sometimes everything is ready for
that rare but definitive composite of "conquering force"
and "unextortable concession" or "a favor of fate."[17] The
hero's virtues are rewarded by good luck at just the right
time and the right place. If "the twofold temporal aspect of
the erotic [is the] momentarily climactic, abruptly subsid-
ing passion, and the idea of something which cannot
pass,"[18] so in the novel of intrigue the reader is led up to
and away from the climax, first with rising fear and expectation, and then with the satisfaction that it was a good
story, worth the time spent reading it. Just as pity and terror
are evoked by tragedy and then a purgation of these pas-
sions somehow achieved, so the reader of the thriller finds
that with a good story he has also gone through some rite
of purification.

Unlike life, which rambles on with many diversions from
birth to death, an adventure is a tidy run from one point to
another with few distractions. There is something in man
which wishes that life itself were as clear, simple, orderly,
definable. It is not. Therefore, we dream. In dreaming we
reorder reality according to our accumulated vision of the
elements that matter. Of course when we come to do this
in writing, or when we read someone else's reordering, we
have to accommodate ourselves to an arbitrary setting for
these nuclear elements: boredom, innocence, evil, chance,
crisis, tension, violence, resolution, courage, endurance,

luck, victory. We read about spies and agents, Berlin and Istanbul, fast cars and machine pistols, Nazis and Communists. These are the necessary and yet quite arbitrary symbols for an excursion into chaos. The symbols work not because they are authentic but because the emotional logic locks in with that of the reader.

Poetic Justice and Tragedy

The thriller takes for granted a world of repressed desires. Unfulfilled may be the better word, for we are too apt to think today that any desire that is unfulfilled is so because it is repressed. Fulfillment may simply be impossible. There are some desires that are too great for us, and neither taboos nor men prevent them. We get pretty much what we want, if we can. Less is denied us by prohibition or taboo than some may think. We have only ourselves and the probabilities of life to blame if we are not all heroes. This does not mean that everything turns out all right. On the contrary, the balance of good and evil in the world has probably not changed at all. Only the forms of evil have changed, and the names of the powers of darkness.

Good does not always triumph over evil, justice is not always done. "It was all very fine to say that Right triumphed . . . in actual practice, Right and Justice were far from infallible."[19] Most thrillers end with respectful homage paid to poetic justice, the justice of the imagination. And yet this is not why thrillers are written. There are thrillers without poetic justice, like John Le Carré's. These are tragic thrillers, closer to the real world than the romantic thrillers. Closer? Or only as close? For surely there is heroism also, and justice done, victories occasionally won in the real world. Why should we not read books that show that too? The main point of a thriller is not the demonstration of some aspect of the world. Rather, the end of the thriller is the demonstration of a personality, the writer's inner life, his apprehension of experience either romantic or ironic, heroic or tragic.

This is why it does not matter in the least whether the fictional world bears any resemblance to the world of history, in particular contemporary history. That is a matter of coincidence, and quite secondary. What should be obvious, however, is that in the middle of the twentieth century the heroic and the tragic sense of life are equally strong and viable, and that from neither point of view must it be held that good always triumphs over evil. Some good always loses; there is always some reason to weep. There is reason to rejoice, too, even in tragedy. This is true even of the end of *The Spy Who Came in from the Cold.* Leamas and Liz have been deceived; both die. But they have seen the deception and protested, and that is more than most people are capable of. Leamas did not trap Mundt, he trapped Fiedler, Mundt's enemy, Fiedler whom Control and Mundt together were using Leamas and Liz to destroy. From the point of view of Control, Leamas had helped to destroy the more dangerous of the two men. From the point of view of individual human worth, he had helped to destroy the better man. Worse, Control's plan anticipated that Liz and Leamas would fall in love, that her love for him would be needed to prove the case against Fiedler, and that knowing too much she would have to die. The reader's gradual understanding of the unfolding of these tragic ironies is always just one step behind Leamas' understanding, until at the end the full realization of perfidy is too much even for Leamas to take in.

John Le Carré seems worlds apart from Buchan: not only the difference between a happy ending and an unhappy ending, the gregarious and patronizing Hannay and the silent and cynical Leamas, but even more the new sophistication of motives. Or should we simply say a tangle, a labyrinth of motives? Geoffrey Household foreshadowed this change in *Rogue Male*, which on one level is a story of a manhunt, and on another level an extended session, under pressure of the manhunt, of self-analysis. On one level Buchan still lives, on the other John Le Carré is born. The hero keeps trying to assure himself that he is a simple man, "not accustomed to inquire very deeply into motives."[20] "My reasons were insistent but frequently obscure."[21] "I was fighting against self-knowledge."[22] "I am ruled by my emotions."[23] He protests too much, and finally his emotions surface and he understands himself as a man out to revenge the murder of the woman he loved. Good God, we say, didn't he know that all along? Perhaps Household was drawing on a stock of highmindedness and phobia of introspection which is peculiar to England. Whether one finds it comical or exasperating depends to a large extent on the degree to which one takes this level of the story seriously. The level of the manhunt is done well enough to preoccupy most readers.

For most contemporary readers it would be enough to be told that the hero wanted to assassinate a dictator—Hitler being the obvious real life model—and no further explanation of motives would be needed. But Household could not do that. To stalk a dictator might be considered sport, but to shoot him would be as sneaky as for a sheriff to gun down a bad man without giving him time to draw first. Evil must be imagined personally in order to justify personal revenge, and even this is tantamount to taking justice into one's own hands. The line to be drawn between this and releasing destructive instincts is too fine for most consciences to draw. Who can tell the real motives of our impulses to hurt or kill? When we try to discover them, we are more likely to find ourselves in the middle of the briar patch.

This is the reason why so many critiques of the thriller suggest that it is "a harmless release of cruelty present in everyone." This may be so, but it seems to me an over-simplification of the thriller, if not a questionable thesis about human nature. Even if Louise Bogan was right in saying that the thriller represents "the breakthrough of the submerged unconscious,"[24] does this necessarily mean that the submerged unconscious is criminal? No one would deny that men are thwarted and injured, insulted and threatened, and that they want to break loose. Nor do we need to deny that in their frustration they cannot imagine any other way to freedom except the way of destruction. But this is not the same as saying that we want to hurt and kill. There is a vast difference between the evil we would do because we are weak, mixed-up, and desperate, and the evil we do because we are strong and calculating. We would be foolish to try to maintain that some men do not have criminal instincts; we would be even more foolish to try to assume that all do. St. Augustine never really stopped being a Manichee, but that is no reason to imitate him. Not every man is torn between two basic instincts, one for good and the other for evil. If we have learned anything recently, we should have taken in the experience of diversity, much as John Le Carré has expressed it:

"We just don't know what people are like, we can never tell; there isn't any truth about human beings, no formula

that meets each one of us. And there are some of us—
aren't there?—who are nothing, who are so labile that we
astound ourselves. . . . The people who are like that—do
you know their secret? They can't feel anything inside
them, no pleasure or pain, no love or hate; they're ashamed
and frightened that they can't feel. And their shame drives
them to extravagance and color."[25]

Even the resemblances that we note between people's behavior and reasoning must always be accepted guardedly.
What is unsaid and unseen, if known, could change our
evaluation completely. It happens all the time. People fool
us. They turn out to be other than we thought. We who
think we have seen everything are continually being disil-
lusioned. Cynicism is no respecter of persons; it is busy
every day laying booby traps for the sophisticated as well
as for the gullible.

After a while disillusionment, like failure, takes its toll.
After a while something really does get repressed, something that the psychologists have not paid much attention
to. Not poetic justice, not the criminal instincts, but something better and simpler, namely, the love of the good itself.
After a while disillusionment enters the emotional machinery as a permanent element called suspicion. After a while,
we do learn a new sophistication of motives, and confuse
this with suspicion of the good. We are no longer able to
believe in anyone's apparently good motives; we have left
the territory of trust altogether. Call it what we will, "the
Victorian world where one knows one's way around," "certain certainties," it is gone, and nothing stable or credible
replaces it. Nevertheless, many of us would still like to
think that

behind the complicated details of the world stand the simplicities: God is good, the grown-up man or woman knows the answer to every question, there is such a thing as truth, and justice is as measured and faultless as a clock. Our heroes are simple: they are brave, they tell the truth, they are good swordsmen and they are never in the long run really defeated . . . a world of great simplicity of which we knew the rules, but the later books are complicated and contradictory with experience.[26]

This is an old-fashioned way of saying what we mean, and we are not old-fashioned, and therefore it is not the best way. We may not want any of these things specifically. We are probably too sophisticated to want them at all. But who would not prefer truth to mirage, firmness to instability? The problem is how to say what we mean without pretending to a simplicity that will never be ours again.

The history of the thriller does not solve this problem, although it may suggest some of the conditions of an answer, giving "a hint of an explanation" rather than an explanation. "Beware of formulas," says Greene. "If there is a God, he's not a God of formulas."[27] Nor is the thriller a philosopher's answer book. It is more like a philosopher's casebook. What we see in this history is the development of a cautious, reflective, even introspective approach to experience without at the same time losing appreciation, along with expectation, of moral idealism. The virtuous man is still to be preferred to the vicious; the change is that we no longer expect that the virtuous man will inevitably either win or survive. If we mourn his passing, we do not forget the importance to us of his example. As long as men scrupulously follow truth wherever it leads them, without at the same time losing their capacity for pity and self-sacrifice, the ideal of conscience has been proved. But when investigation and inquiry are practiced only as a game, or are put at the service of ends that we are unwilling or unable to judge, then truth is barren and its servant only a shell of a man. When the hero of the thriller is only a functionary, we may read the book for the sake of secondary sensations or for an exposure to a factual world—foreign places, luxury, debauchery, intelligence procedures—but not for the pleasure of observing free human beings.

Thriller Truth

As long as the thriller retains its concern for truth, whether romantic or tragic, it will be worth reading. But what kind of truth are we talking about? "The truth," thinks Scobie in *The Heart of the Matter*, "has never been of any real value to any human being—it is a symbol for mathematicians and philosophers to pursue. In human relations kindness and lies are worth a thousand truths."[28] Scobie found that neither kindness nor lies could keep him from getting so tangled up with contradictory loyalties that the only way out was suicide. Was he being kind to his wife or his mistress in getting out of their way? Who can tell? Perhaps kindness should not be the criterion of behavior in any case. It certainly is not one that a man can depend on. Scobie to the end told the truth to himself, as much as he could know, probably as much as any man could have known in his situation. We cannot blame him for that. Of course, he did not tell others all he knew, and he does not differ from most of us in that either. He never supposed that there is no truth or that it does not matter whether one keeps straight what truth is available. If Scobie did not abase himself before truth, it was because he valued something else more highly, the subordination of truth to well-being. This is what preoccupied Nietzsche in *Beyond Good and Evil*: "Granted that we want the truth: why not rather untruth? And uncertainty? Even ignorance?"[29] And he replied by saying, "The question is how far an opinion is life-furthering, life-preserving, species-preserving, perhaps species-rearing; and we are fundamentally inclined to maintain that the falsest opinions are the most indispensable to us; that without a recognition of logical fictions . . . man could not live."[30] This answer is not final, at least not for all of us. Sometimes we are forced to ask another question, namely, how we can know what is life-furthering, life-preserving? Is it so easy? Do we not need to be able to distinguish between what appears to be life-furthering and what actually is? Do we not need to ask what is meant by life-furthering, and whether life-preserving is an absolute? How can we do this if we have given up the habit of looking for and speaking the truth? Nietzsche, like Scobie, may have had an attractive idea, but he had not anticipated the difficulties.

If somehow a man could keep in balance to the end of his days a respect for truth and the freedom to use it, there would be more hope for the future of man. But respect requires constant practice, and constant practice not only nurtures habit, it encourages scrupulosity and rigidity. Freedom unveils a vision of endless horizons, with room enough and time enough to contain all distinctions. Few men ever combine both satisfactorily. This is one of the main virtues of the thriller; at best, it does manage. In the thriller the hero cannot remain free unless he discovers the truth, about his predicament, about his enemies, friends, and himself. He cannot discover the truth unless his mind is free. He ceases to be a real human being, to say nothing of a hero, if he is brainwashed. The modern world has thought up many ways to diminish man, and the thriller is one way we have to affirm our belief in a human nature that, while menaced on all sides, has not withered beyond recognition or admiration.

Dread

See how many and what great dangers surround and confront us! Taboos and prohibitions, and the consequent repressions. Enemies that promise us freedom if we forgo truth. Enemies that offer us truth at the cost of freedom. Misunderstanding and violence, indifference and over-concern. Pressures and many-ness, the sheer horror of suffocating many-ness. The world is too much with us. We are afraid of others, we are afraid of ourselves. Others seem to wish us evil; we wish them evil in turn. There is no letup in this war; perhaps there is no good in the human heart either. Is that what causes our instability on the one hand, and our never-ending anxiety on the other? "What restlessness of soul, Lady, has come upon me since I heard you speak, what a tumult of mind!"[31] So spoke Oedipus to Jocasta. He had begun to suspect that the killer he was looking for was himself, that he had married his victim's widow, his own mother.

No doubt there is some measure of guilt mixed with our restlessness. Need we assume that there is nothing but guilt, or, further, that this is the deepest explanation of the restlessness that is the motive behind the world of the thriller? How could we even suggest this? Very easily, for the experience of restlessness is widespread and intense, and is evidence of a void in expectation and trust that nothing promises to fill. If a man feels he has transgressed, he might experience the disjunction between his action and his ideal in terms of a void. Because we cannot live with a void, we turn here and there, waiting for what has been torn apart to be mended. If we have lost the ideal itself, we may also experience the void in the same way. Only by the closest look at experience can we tell the difference between guilt and loss of meaning. Max Picard's imaginative analysis of the phenomenon of deep anxiety takes for granted a religious view of the nature of man, and yet we should not dismiss as nonsensical or irrelevant his suggestion that, having fled from God, man has substituted dread, which is the sense of having no trust in oneself.[32]

The fact is, contemporary men have done just this: they have fled from God and yet have astonishingly little confidence in themselves. Has man substituted dread for God? Not as something to worship, but as his horizon? Substitute the word "trust" for "God" and it may be easier to accept the emotional substitution of dread for God. "Dread is everywhere."[33] If God is everywhere, we do not feel it anymore. Picard, parodying Marx, speaks of man as "an appendage of Dread."[34] And the thriller takes the place of lives of the saints for contemporary man.

Out in the Cold

Perhaps now we can understand better why the thriller is an interesting genre. Not because espionage or security services are new—in fact, they are not—but because they supply something we now need that mankind was given in different forms in the past. When man trusts in God, then the best models of human endeavor and endurance are those men whose trust in God and love for mankind never utterly fail. Their endurance proves the sincerity if not the validity of their belief. In our world (and it is interesting to note that the heroes of Greene's "entertainments" are not believers), where belief is at best uncertain, we are reassured by the ability of the hero to stand alone, without faith or even, in most cases, family. The question is, what will this man do with his solitude? And it is ultimate solitude that he has been introduced to by chance and violence. What resources will he find within himself? Will he be able to persuade people and nature to accommodate themselves to him to the point of providing him avenues of escape? On the one hand, the prospect is not good; for one used to the assurance of living in a friendly environment, the thriller situation is bleak and frightening. We know that already, or we would not have started reading. On the other hand, the prospect is good, for it is the only prospect there ever has been, and now we know it. When we endured before, we thanked God. When we went under, we blamed ourselves or others. Now we know that we are on our own. What we do not yet know is what we own. Will we find out by going out into the cold? This is the problem of the thriller.

There is yet another possibility, anticipated by Picard: "Man cannot stand a continual waiting for a surprise attack of the terrible in the enormous space of Dread."[35] Therefore he goes out into the cold to meet it. Is he really then meeting anything more than shadows of himself, slivers of himself shaved off and lying around? The evil that "fill[s] the emptiness of Dread,"[36] the wish to be God himself, the tension of his own conflicts and failures, the medley of motives, the collection of identities? It is not difficult for the unconscious to suggest a fictional world where all these elements of one man portray a situation in which a man is expected to sort things out and find his integrity through action. And yet action is the one thing that has proved impossible. That is why a man finds himself reading a book which, while insulting his intelligence, goes even further and lays his self-respect low by seducing his emotions. Something is very wrong, he thinks. He is right, something is wrong; he has become part of a conspiracy on the part of history to make man mad.

Picard's analysis of the flight of man from God leads to God as a divine pursuer whom man cannot escape. Flight and dread are symptoms of hysteria, a compulsive escape that brings God nearer the faster man flees. It is certainly debatable that this can be demonstrated. We can as easily guess that the impulse to juxtapose such opposites as the Flight and the Pursuer is one more symptom of the hysterical desperation of the flight. Whether hysterical or not, Picard's theory is one way of living with the many symptoms of mistrust and tension in our world. The thriller may get to the point before long when it will no longer show us examples of moral discernment and integrity, but it is still one of the very few ways the modern world has found even to try, and not forget lessons already learned.

Outside the Law

In its beginnings in Childers, Buchan, and Household the spy thriller was written by rugged individualists for would-be rugged individualists. Or so it seemed. The extreme examples of self-reliance, of an unwillingness to seek official help that bordered on stupidity, are a far cry from the more recent pictures of the dependence of loners on their organizations. Richard Hannay's attitude is the epitome of heroism cut down to British size:

> Here was I a very ordinary fellow, with no particular brains, and yet I was convinced that somehow I was needed to help this business through—that without me it would all go to blazes. I told myself it was sheer silly conceit, that four or five of the cleverest people living, with all the might of the British Empire at their back, had the job in hand. It seemed as if a voice kept speaking in my ear, telling me to be up and doing, or I would never sleep again.[37]

We recognize here the Pelagian spirit, the inner light, the self-righteousness that muddles through. How could anyone like that not succeed? He would never know he had failed. No doubt there is something of Hannay in most of us; we are Hannays *manqués*. But are we really meant to be, or is this wish to be champion only a symptom of an underdeveloped personality? The Hannay syndrome, so to speak, may be similar to the attraction violence has for us, the short cut to dream away frustration.

Buchan seems to have been quite aware of the unfortunate impression his hero might be making. After all, an Englishman should never boast about himself. He could only be allowed to go so far as to say that "every man at the bottom of his heart believes that he is a born detective,"[38] without assuming that any Englishman could be a great detective. (It is ironic that the English of all people, with their passion for privacy, should be so fascinated by the uncovering of privacy.) Buchan seems to have realized that his ebullient hero might be mistaken for a bounder. Why else should he make him repeat his apologia pro vita sua? "I wasn't any kind of Sherlock Holmes. But I have always fancied I had a kind of instinct about questions like this. I don't know if I can explain myself, but I used to use my brains as far as they went, and after they came to a blank wall I guessed, and I usually found my guesses pretty right."[39] The explanation, however, hardly allays the suspicion. Buchan seems to have had an uneasy conscience about Hannay, for he brings the subject up again. "There might be something in the case too delicate for the police to handle."[40] In other words, "the law is an ass," and Hannay is superior to the law. The law is sometimes an ass, of course, and sometimes a knave too. But the man who takes matters as dangerous as these in his own hands without even appealing to the law is a bigger ass. Except in thrillers; there he is called the hero.

Obviously the thriller is not concerned with matters of prudence any more than with legal proprieties and provisions. The thriller appeals directly to the reader's dream of decisive, successful action in a situation of significance beyond his own destiny. He has every right to that dream. In all probability it will remain only a dream, for his own life is unlikely ever to present him with a situation of significance beyond his own fate. It is amazing how anonymous most of us are from birth to death, how far removed from the fuse box, to say nothing of the main power line. We might just as well not have existed at all. Helpless, unknown, and unremembered, most human beings, however sensitive, idealistic, intelligent, go through life as passengers rather than chauffeurs. Although we may pretend that it is the chauffeur who is the social inferior, not those he drives around, most of us, like Toad of Toad Hall, would not mind a turn at the wheel ourselves. No doubt, like

Toad, we too would smash the motorcar, but that would be in real life, not in dream life. Here in our dreams we can do as we please, and there is no question but that we would be pleased to be Hannay rather than Leamas. The latter is too close for comfort, and only the tragic emotional progress from terror to pity to purgation can make Leamas' life and fate bearable. Tragedy needs sympathy—some kind of identification made and then broken—but it needs detachment as well from beginning to end. If we can learn from tragedy, we might be able to learn even to retain a lingering fondness for the old-fashioned hero, or at least for the old-fashioned dream of being a hero. It is a good dream, even if it never meets its double in real life.

Real Life and Ideal Life

Fleming's biographer, John Pearson, has called the Bondiad an "experiment in the autobiography of dreams,"[41] and his documentation of the similarities between Fleming and Bond is very persuasive. Perhaps what he has done for Fleming could be done with other thriller characters and their authors. It is not in the fictional character's actions that one seeks an analogy, but in what the author himself most admires. It is easy to imagine Greene's little review of Buchan being extended into a book-length treatment of that writer. Indeed, it is probably much easier to find such analogies in romantic than in tragic fiction. The ironic perspective needed for the latter is alien to dreams. For this reason we should be reluctant to call thriller literature as a whole "escape literature." Even so, the relations between real life and fiction, the daydream and the night dream, real adventures and imagined adventures, are too close to justify defining the varieties of thriller writing in those terms.

Real life is the trouble. Anyone who tries to write either biography or autobiography knows the difficulties. In the first place, after you have noted the two fixed limits of birth and death—and if you are writing about yourself you do only half of that—you are faced with the problem of where to begin, what to include, and what to leave out. Real life is an undigested, probably indigestible mass of facts, some known and some unknown, that only an arbitrary hand would dare to arrange in any strict chronological order. If everything is important, and who of us ever thinks that, then a retelling is impossible. If only some things are important, then which ones, and how are you to find the criteria of importance, and even if you do, then how are you to find the facts that fit them?

In comparison, the imagination, of historian or novelist, proposes an ideal life that has a course of some definable importance, with clear beginning and end and a finite number of contributing facts. Whereas in real life a person's movements take place much of the time without perceptible and separate decisions being made, in an ideal life each moment is anticipated and recorded as part of a decision-making process that marks off the human from the animal. Whereas in real life so much that goes on is admittedly trivial and arbitrary, unnecessary and unmemorable, in the ideal life of the imagination everything is evaluated according to its worth. So in real life days and weeks go by without an individual being able to say he has done anything worth living for, while in an ideal life a man puts all he has behind the pursuit of some excellence, and when that is achieved he admits with satisfaction that he has been fulfilling his destiny. He has discovered his integrity through what he has done and can tell himself that he is what he is because he freely willed it. Further, his life will not leave others untouched. In Max Frisch's words, he will have left "a deposit."[42] But, as Frisch concluded, "It's precisely the disappointing stories, which have no proper ending and therefore no proper meaning, that sound true to life."[43]

Dream Life

In such a way, sadly, we acknowledge the difference between real life and ideal life. There are only two general alternatives to real life: real adventures and imaginary adventures. For what I have been calling ideal life is really an adventurous life of one kind or another, a life torn loose from the continuum of life (perhaps more accurately called the agglomeration) and yet it is related to its center. We do not expect this to happen except by chance, and this is how fate and adventure begin to be related. Whether the adventure is a failure or a success will also depend on contingency; for just as it may be true that a successful agent needs luck and speculation, so a successful adventurer of any kind always needs both luck and freedom. In a sense an adventure, real or imagined, is a kind of escape from a movement through life that gives no deep satisfactions; it is only when the land to which we escape is a kind of never-never-land of wishing, call it romantic if you will, that a complete transition takes place and the term "escape" is fully justified. When we burrow down beneath the surface of our normal confusions and disquietudes and trace the root system of what is on the surface, the process should not be called escape at all, but a re-presentation of the real.

The human spirit has three alternatives to accepting real life, if life itself has not become an adventure, and if we do not expect it to: daydreams, fiction, and night dreams. They all involve "the juxtaposition of fantasy with reality."[44] Nicholas Blake (C. Day Lewis) has said that the thriller writer "can put unreal characters into realistic situations, or he can put realistic characters into fantastic situations."[45] This is what most writers have done. But life is just as fantastic as fiction—sometimes more so—and it is probably just as true to say that any character can have a real counterpart, and there is no fictional situation that cannot be duplicated in fact. The definitive feature of the dream world is not that it is fantastic or improbable, even though something about it may appear so. What is remarkable is that dreams, deliberate or spontaneous, like fiction, concentrate on happenings that seem crucial. If they are spontaneous, as at night, we are in the dark as to their meaning as well; they need some kind of interpretation to become clear. If they are part of a habit of daydreaming, the chances are that we have dreamed them before many times and know why only too well. "One could laugh at day-dreams, but so long as you had the capacity to day-dream, there was a chance that you might develop some of the qualities of which you dreamed."[46] When real life takes over, the daydreams usually cease, for their usefulness is over. No one is more surprised by this than the daydreamer.

There is one commonly experienced feature of both daydreams and the dreams of the unconscious, the paralysis that occurs before the completion of some crucial act. We try to walk out of a room and cannot. We try to free ourselves from numbness and cannot. We try to touch someone and can only reach out. The intention and the meaning are there, also the effort; it is the doing that is impossible. "In a dream you cannot escape: the feet are lead-weighted;

you cannot stir from before the ominous door which almost imperceptibly moves. It is the same in life: sometimes it is more difficult to make a scene than to die."[47] We bring the binding frustrations of life right into our dreams. The result is that while the dream points to a good way out of the frustration, it does not attempt to fool us into forgetting the frustration. This is as true of daydreams as of night dreams: they too can be honest. Joseph Conrad probably meant something like this when he said that "perhaps life is just that . . . a dream and a fear."[48] We dream because we fear we will not really live. We carry the fear right through the dream to the end of the dream, an end that, like real life, is no end at all, but only a new source of frustration.

Of course, there are dreams that end happily. There are happy thrillers and unhappy thrillers. We can get what we pay for, and we buy what we think we can consume. We may be looking for objective correlatives of our desires, enjoying improbabilities because we are bored with probabilities. Or we may welcome the opportunity to explore the maze of our inner workings whose unclean obscurity we are not unfamiliar with. The world of the thriller is far more inclusive than most of its critics have admitted. It has a greater claim on a serious man's study, by way of entertainment, than serious men have acknowledged. Although the plots and their environments, and most of the figures in the landscape, are more banal than sensational (we are so often disappointed by the advertising), the progression of the central characters in, through, and out of crises gives each reader a chance to bring his own relationship to crisis out into the open. As he follows, then involves himself emotionally with the hero's emotions, he will isolate from his own life whatever is unfulfilled or not fully understood. When this happens, the reader has, by means of an excursion into chaos, taken a trip to freedom as well, and is the better man for it.

Probably most of us have had the unsettling experience of discovering that, just as in some dull moment of real life we wish we were away on some adventure, so to our astonishment in the middle of an adventure we wish for the normality of real life. We would not have thought this possible. Such was the experience of Arthur Rowe, as he accompanied police through the night on their way to foil a Nazi plot:

Over there among the unknown tribes a woman was giving birth, rats were nosing among sacks of meal, an old man was dying, two people were seeing each other for the first time by the light of a lamp: everything in that darkness was of such deep importance that their errand could not equal it —this violent superficial chase, this cardboard adventure hurtling at forty-five miles an hour along the edge of the profound natural common experiences of men. Rowe felt a longing to get back into that world: into the world of homes and children and quiet love and the ordinary unspecified fears and anxieties the neighbour shared.[49]

The professional agent may become used to the improbable. The dreamer supposes he can too. But when the improbable takes place, we sometimes find that it is not what we want at all. It is "cardboard" and faintly ridiculous. Of course, it may be dangerous too, and few of us would care to put up with nervous tension and uncertainty without let-up. The suspense of vicarious experience can always be abandoned, in the middle of reading or viewing, if it is too much for us. After all, it is only a story. " 'Don't you see that if things like that happened, life would be quite different. One would have to begin over again.' "[50] Do we really want that? Or do we want our adventures safe and cheap?

It may well be that there is another explanation, one that is not so embarrassing. When we anticipate satisfaction from dream or fiction, only to discover that the thrill makes us yearn for the tranquillity that formerly bored us, we may be discovering that both dream and reality are necessary and mutually dependent modes of experience. We cannot get along without both, and our mistake is to assume that one is more important than the other. They may be meant to witness to each other and merge with each other, making a whole man. When we tire of one, there is the other to fall back on or, to use the language of the thriller, to escape to. It is just this readiness to talk of escape that blinds us to the other side of the experience of flight, namely, the search for ourselves. If we do not feel we have found ourselves at the end of each flight, then we can always go back and start over again.

THE READER:
His Secret World

Subjective Correlatives

Perhaps more than any other genre the thriller is about ourselves. We read about men in crisis, and attend them as they stand up to danger, and finally come out to a place of safety and self-knowledge. Their tales are told as objectively as fiction knows how. Their worlds are self-contained and explicit. We know their environments; and in a brief time we get to know the men themselves. Sometimes they change before our eyes. They find out things about themselves they had not known before. Sometimes we take comfort in their stability and dependability. "Thou art a rock." We may think we are reading about other people. In fact, we are reading about ourselves.

As we read we may learn many things that we had taken for granted, such as the faces and behavior of heroes. We had not suspected someone so drab, so unreflecting, or so uncommunicative could be so interesting, let alone heroic. We thought we knew all there is to know about crises: world crises, national crises, emotional crises, religious crises. But we had never been in a crisis in which everything we are and own was put on the line. We had not experienced that concentrate of danger, isolation, and tension that is the lot of one who is on the run. We thought we knew what it is to want to escape from boredom, but we had not yet found that escape from something is often just a cover for a voyage toward something. The truth is we had not fully realized that behind the subject of the stories we read are the correlatives of ourselves. They are subjects, not yet objective. They lurk in silence and in secret below the cover of our avowed interest in fiction.

Secret Adventures

The fictional subject of the thriller differs from the heroes of other adventures not only because he is both hunter and hunted, but because of a transformation of identity that must take place when he elects to take on evil singlehanded. Not only do we call this kind of adventure a chase, we must go further and call it a secret adventure. The delight that a reader takes in following this adventure is aimed in large part at the secrecy, even more than at the crisis itself and the efforts of the hero to win. Some people appear to find secrecy fascinating in itself.

A secret is a truth withheld. If we wish to know something and find ourselves within its presence, and do not know it as it is, we are in the ambience of a secret truth held back. If we wait for truth to be released, or wait until we can force it to show itself, we are said to be in suspense. The tension of suspense is distinctive, but it is not in itself responsible for that special thrill which goes along with the thriller. That response is a concern for the fundamental tampering of the human personality, namely, the remaking of identity itself. This in turn is not a thrill evoked by the unknown, but the excitement set in motion by the unhinging of the one thing in human existence that we think we can count on, namely, the central nature and stability of the self. The quality, therefore, of the delight evoked by a successful thriller is a mixed one, the exhilaration of freedom combined with fear and dizziness before the potential loss of self altogether.

As if this were not enough, there is still more. The self that is unhinged, as it were, is only in part the self of the fictional hero; to some degree it is always the reader's self as well, who has decided, for the space of his reading, to "put off the old man" and "put on the new." In this way, secret life is intertwined with secret life; the rapt attention paid to one is being paid to the other also. But there is a difference. We do not need to show that we are aware of our own uncertain calling; we may in fact be quite unaware. It is enough that unconsciously we permit the mind to attach itself to stories of other men's transformations of their identities. The depth of our reaction will measure the challenge that is being presented indirectly to our hidden view of ourselves.

Cover

Every thriller hero sooner or later must hide himself. If he does not, he will be caught, and if caught, he not only will have lost the chance to become a savior, but he may lose his life as well. On his use of his identity everything depends. This is the true sense of the crisis in the thriller. Not the nature of tension, or of danger or violence, not the quality of isolation, but the search for a new life through a new identity. The way of the thriller is not the way of the moralist; it is secret, not open. The hero employs ruses and disguises. He can change his name, his appearance, his history, his beliefs, his allegiances. He can even disappear altogether, or go into hiding. He will not become a nothing. Even an agent who has been given a number instead of a name, a number to cover his name, has just traded one identity for another. Which is the real one? Both are real, of course; they have different functions. His old identity, however little he shows it in public, will be one he can never completely shake loose from, so far as he himself is concerned. He will constantly have to keep it from coming to the surface and contradicting his new identity. He can have as many covers as he needs. This means that whenever he wishes to conceal his actions or their purposes, he will assume an identity that at the very least does not even suggest concealment. The best cover, therefore, is simply to be oneself, one's real self.

What is it, however, to be one's real self? For the purposes of concealment, it hardly matters. All that matters is that other people take you for granted. You may be in agony over who and what you are, but so long as you seem to be the person other people expect you to be, your inner life is irrelevant. Nevertheless, the question is important to ourselves, even if not to someone else. For one thing, there is always a risk of losing touch with an identity that has either been repressed over a long period of time or that has never been defined and stabilized at any time. If such a thing should take place, either the psyche will react with a demoralization that makes it impossible to maintain a cover, or the self will cease to be a self and become an automaton, at the beck and call of masters. A computerized or brainwashed agent (*The Manchurian Candidate*) is neither impossible nor unknown.

Richard Hannay could never have doubted his own identity. On the one occasion an enemy tried to hypnotize him, he resisted successfully:

I have been told more than once by doctors who dabbled in the business that I was the most hopeless subject for hypnotism that they ever struck. One of them once said that I was about as unsympathetic as Table Mountain. I must suppose that the intractable bedrock of commonplaceness in me now met the something which was striving to master me and repelled it. I felt abominably helpless, my voice was not my own, my eyes were tortured and aching, but I had recovered my mind.[1]

Nor could the British agent in *The Ipcress File* be deceived into thinking he had been flown to Hungary, when all the time he was being held prisoner in England. A cover is intended to protect the self or to mislead someone else. Someone else may also try to wipe out the basic self on which our power to distinguish reality from appearance depends. Even if we do not always recognize the importance of this self, those who wish to make use of us do. For some men the attempt to subvert them is just enough to make them take themselves seriously for the first time.

In a thriller a man must hide for a variety of reasons: to keep out of trouble, until he decides to pick up the challenge; to escape from trouble, once trouble has become his business; to divert attention from himself; to give the crisis a chance to quiet down; to draw off attention from those more important than himself, as he himself is being hunted down. There are two widely differing choices—dropping out of sight altogether or moving among one's enemies with a changed identity. Richard Hannay in *The Thirty-Nine Steps* tries to hide by disguising himself, not once but several times, and leaving London by train for Scotland. When he is discovered crossing the moors, he realizes that he must keep moving, assuming different names, clothes, and occupations. Finally his cover is blown, in the house of his enemy. He escapes but only to be tricked again by the superior talent his opponent has for assuming new identities also. If the amateur is defeated by the professional at the game of disguises, the fledgling detective, stretching credibility, proves to be more competent than the seasoned spy. Never mind plausibility, it is virtue that really counts, the stability and honesty of the basic self. This is a comforting view, and in itself a cover concealing the harsh realities of life.

Buried Selves

There are also human beings who, having failed in life, gradually drop out of sight, fade away, and are forgotten even while they are still alive. Dr. Dick Diver in F. Scott Fitzgerald's *Tender Is the Night* is a pathetic case in point. There are others who, weary of the conflicts and tensions of existence, finally prefer to be freed from responsibilities and all the attending nexus of pressures and cares. There are those (like Max Frisch's Stiller) who would like to be able to reject the past completely and start life all over with an identity not subject to other people's definitions. They would use a transformation of name and an assumed past to free them to look for a new center and identity. Then, of course, there are the run-of-the-mill agents and spies who have lost contact with law and custom because they have been lured into a situation which appears to tell against them. A new, and, from their point of view, false identity has been forced on them. Their isolation cruelly deprives them of even the secret comfort of knowing that their real selves are approved by the permanent inhabitants of their former world.

At the center of their isolation such people experience the emotions of their secrecy, outside law and expectation. They must be perpetually on guard against the discovery of their deception, for even a cover that is meant to protect must do so by deceiving. Balancing what they remember of themselves with what they have assumed, they soon learn to know a tension different from any hitherto experienced. Always the pull back to reality, alternating with the pull toward the success of their task or the security of their position. Tension, tautness, in the end fatigue so depressing and chronic that they approach the snapping point. When this is reached, then comes paralysis or a splintering or nauseating vertigo. And yet when the tension is fresh, it is welcomed with exhilaration as a sign of a new integration of the personality. All systems are working at full throttle, at highest pitch.

This dialectic of tension is the reason for the ambiguity of cover. As it wears thin and becomes vulnerable to being blown, the earlier excitement is lost, never to be regained, even by professionals who know what to expect each time. To the amateur, on the other hand, there is an excitement beyond the heightening of sensitivity and awareness, and that is the delight that can be felt on the rim of the unexpected. When the unforeseen is outside the law, the fact that it is at complete odds with normal living promotes a sweet and strange delight. For some it may well be that a repressed—covered—longing to savor evil is the cause. For others it will be sufficient that the unforeseen is simply taken as a symptom of a lost freedom to go where one would and do what one has finally been able to do.

Thrillers provide easy lessons for those who have something to hide. Their possible abuse is far from the intention of the writer who ostensibly is concerned with the protection of a good man and a good society. The end seems always to justify these means, and the question is usually not raised as to whether the means themselves are shameful. Presented as ways of self-disclosure, they seem appropriate to that end, whether their purpose is to protect good from evil or to protect evil itself. Who tells everyone everything he knows about himself? Some do not tell all they know to anyone. Although their secretiveness may exasperate and insult other people, they have a right to disclose only as much of themselves as they wish. We judge them harmless, if unfriendly, as long as they are not trying to hurt us or to keep from us what is rightfully ours. There are some who do not mean to withhold themselves, but do not know as much of themselves as those around them. And yet we do not accuse them of anything more than blindness.

The Rules of Deception

Only when the rules for maintaining cover (in plain language, deceiving) are laid out on the table, does the moral sense experience twinges. The twinges are often considerable. Ashenden was an amateur, but he learned quickly. "It was Ashenden's principle ... to tell as much of the truth as he conveniently could."[2] For those who want from their fellow men the whole truth and nothing but the truth, this maxim for behavior is not very satisfactory. There is something a little disturbing and sneaky about the word "conveniently." It suggests the possibility of a conflict of interest between us and those who appear to be telling the truth but who in fact are not. We doubt whether truth is truth if it is not complete. Sadly, it is as true as truth can be, for at all times truth is incomplete, whether by intention or by ignorance. Ashenden's principle has variations that make it easily adaptable to almost any situation calling for concealment. We might speak of this as the principle of the false track.

In this way fair play is respected. If the larger part of what is shown or said is true, the smaller part is not only false but is also out in the open for anyone with eyes to see. All the clues are always present. All suspicious strangers have to do is catch a glimpse of the inevitable disproportion between truth and falsehood. Take Ashenden's own variation of this. "It was curious . . . how he was able to combine real emotion with false fact."[3] With certain people, and in certain situations, what is important and noticeable is the emotion of the man, and not the accompanying words. If someone seems sincere, particularly if he has been on the level with us in the past, we are inclined to believe him and not look for inconsistencies of behavior. We usually judge the man, not his words or actions. The man sometimes changes, and then only his words and actions provide any clue to his new character.

The irony of Leamas' being used in order to hide the real intentions of his own superior by no means undercuts the very principle used against him and which he embodied so efficiently. "The qualities he exhibited to Fiedler, the restless uncertainty, the protective arrogance concealing shame, were not approximations but extensions of qualities he actually possessed."[4] This is not Ashenden's balancing of sincerity with false fact, but the forging of a new character by building on some of the strengths and weaknesses of the basic self. This is why we can say that while a new self is being fabricated, "cover should never be fabricated but only an extension of the truth."[5] Cover is the fabric of the new man, and the difference between the old man and the new is qualitative.

There are other variations. A cover story can be convincing if one tells the truth about many things that are obvious, but not about the one truth that is the mark of a new departure. By lie or by suppression, the cover is kept intact. Or, all facts may be admitted, but with an interpretation that diverts attention from some compromising new direction. One thing above all is needed, to live the part as if it were the only part. "There was that other maxim of Peter's which had helped me when I had been a roadman. 'If you are playing a part, you will never keep it up unless you convince yourself that you are it.' "[6] Perhaps on the stage this maxim can produce an impression of reality and immediacy that one associates only with great actors. The toll it takes from the emotional mechanism of the actor is incalculable. When the play is over, the act may go on. After playing many roles, personality becomes so splintered (Ingmar Bergman's *Persona*) that it no longer seems worthwhile being a person at all. As for the man on the run who needs a cover, he can learn to play a part well and still be tripped up by meeting someone from his former world. "How difficult it was never to make [a slip]. Ashenden must be on his guard."[7] To be on guard is just what you cannot do if you have submerged your basic self in the part. To do that is to obliterate the natural, conscious split between one and the other. Because it is natural, it is almost impossible to do, at least for any length of time. Sooner or later, fatigue or shock sets in, and all can be lost in one second of faltering. No one is ever really above suspicion.

On Being Exposed

If the actor or the agent does not realize the instability of his role, the reader of a thriller—and the spectator in the theater far more—is always aware of the risks. The agent may be exposed. He will make a slip. He will become scared and fall apart. The reader waits for the practically inevitable. He knows that the writer in this instance will usually be willing to subject the hero to further danger, an ultimate trap, in order to demonstrate his ingenuity in springing him. The writer may have a nobler reason than that. He may respect the risks involved in maintaining cover and feel he must demonstrate his appreciation of probabilities so that he cannot be ridiculed as a fantasy maker. If it is fantastic to permit someone to keep his cover, it is more fantastic to show him escaping a trap once the cover has been blown. Unless a writer is prepared to write tragedy, however, he will have to free his hero from disaster sooner or later.

When circumstances permit, or actors wish to exhibit their versatility, it sometimes happens that one man finds himself acting more than one role at a time. In the world of espionage such a man is a double agent. He plays for both sides; each side thinks he plays for it alone. Sometimes neither side knows that he plays for the other; in that case he is in himself neutral, with no loyalty to anyone but himself. In most cases, the double agent is faithful to one side and pretends to be faithful to the other in order to thwart it or get important secrets from it. Although double agents know what they are doing, the juggling of roles that is such a constant in their lives lays such a heavy strain on the nerves that "it's just a matter of time before they lose their grip on reality. They begin to drown in a sea of confusion."[8] Although they may be tempted to run away, if they have any common sense they will know that "it's no good running away. [They] know that and keep repeating it to [themselves] every day."[9] There is nowhere to run.

Wherever the hunted man runs, it is possible for someone to find him. He does not even have the respite after performance that the actor can look forward to, unless he has surrendered himself completely to his role. The spy when he is alone is no better off than when he is out among men. Solitude is his most dangerous hour.

A man who lives a part, not to others but alone, is exposed to obvious psychological dangers. In itself, the practice of deception is not particularly exacting; it is a matter of experience, of professional *expertise*; it is a facility most of us can acquire. But while a confidence trickster, a play-actor or a gambler can return from his performance to the ranks of his admirers, the secret agent enjoys no such relief. For him, deception is first a matter of self-defense. He must protect himself not only from without but from within, and against the most natural of impulses.[10]

What he must above all steel himself against is "the fracture beneath that glassy surface."[11] The outward slip indicates that an inner fracture has occurred, one that can only seldom be mended. If the slip goes unnoticed, all may not be lost. If the slip is noticed, and the time of arrest seems inevitable, only the very brave will continue to be able to put a good face on things. The rest crumple, face and body, all. When the false role is exposed, the real man, if he is still inside, will appear, but naked, vulnerable. Having put his confidence in his role and his ability to sustain it, having given his life to this task, he finds that failure can annihilate self-confidence. All is lost. Or is all lost? Will he get some comfort from his return from the territory of lies to the place of truth?

The Moral Burden

When all is said and done, this is what thriller adventures must be reduced to, adventures in lying. In *The Looking-Glass War* there is a passage in which an ambitious intelligence officer mentions to the undersecretary of his ministry his need for a cover story for a proposed operation. The latter remarks, " 'Cover story? Ah yes: a lie.' " And the narrator adds, "He was a churchman and disliked irregular things."[12] Some men enjoy conspiracy for its own sake, "the Great Game." Some, more high-minded, are pleased to be given any chance to serve their country. Say it as you will, cover means lie, deception, a deliberately misleading, avoiding, twisting, tampering with the truth. In fact, to be a good agent a man has to do more than tell lies, he must live a lie, by pretending to an allegiance he does not always feel, and by pretending to be someone he is not. For some men this imposes a moral burden they can never fully accustom themselves to carrying.

For others the problems are quite different. The most common is the risk they run, the longer they lie and pretend, of becoming entangled in their untruth, so that they not only slip up, but worse, lose touch with what is true and real. " 'Damn it, madam,' " he exploded, " 'Don't you have any instinct for what's true or what's false? Can't you tell you're being lied to?' "[13] When everything becomes a lie, there is nothing left to use as a criterion for truth. The liar himself can be deceived by lies. So will the man who has taught others to lie. "You teach them to cheat, to cover their tracks, and they cheat you as well."[14] The net of espionage has then become a network of lies in which the master himself becomes slave of his slaves. Nothing but tragedy can be expected in such a world, for sooner or later the honest men are used by the dishonest, the best by the worst. Only spectators and readers have any chance at all of escaping with their honesty intact. And they may have had a very close shave.

The reader who feels he is, at this point, beginning to learn a harsh lesson from thrillers may well be asking whether the risks that must be taken by their heroes are worth it. Sooner or later, exceptions only prove the rule, and it would be imprudent to recommend living under a cover as a prescription for a good life. Most would-be adventurers would either be used or caught, and if they escaped from external harm they would be running the risk of becoming entangled in their own professional deceptions. Unless they can afford to carry with them moral scruples inherited from a well-ordered and peaceful existence, they will be forced by the logic of danger to accept to some degree the maxim "Everything is lawful, in espionage as in love and war." Necessity makes new virtues or simply dulls the sting of conscience.

The thriller reader is, in any case, in much the same position as Gyges the Lydian shepherd, whose good fortune Plato describes in *The Republic*. One day he found a dead body, and a gold ring on one of its fingers. He put the ring on his own hand, and when by chance he turned the bezel inward he discovered that he was invisible to his companions. Plato then asks what would happen if any of us had such a ring, and his answer is:

No one, it is commonly believed, would have such iron strength of mind as to stand fast in doing right or keep his hands off other men's goods, when he could go to the market-place and fearlessly help himself to anything he wanted, enter houses and sleep with any woman he chose, set prisoners free and kill men at his pleasure, and in a word go about among men with the powers of a God.[15]

The likelihood is that different men would want to do different things, and some would be harmful to others and some would not. Much that we would do is presently forbidden. And yet this does not mean that we would do that which is unlawful because we wanted to break the law or because we wanted to do evil. In most instances we would simply be doing something that we had already wanted to do and for one reason or another could not. We would be attracted to particular experiences and the novelty of these experiences. So thriller readers on the whole are interested in vicarious experience mainly because it is new to them, untasted, not because it may be illicit. Only when a reader discovers that he enjoys sadism instead of being horrified should he become concerned about the morality of his reading.

The Real Self

There are so many occasions in the course of reading a thriller when I may ask who I am. Am I the torturer or the victim? The answer sometimes comes out more slowly and uncertainly than we might expect. Am I the hero, and at which time of his life? Before anything happens to him, when we have just met and he is still moving around openly and easily in the world we are both used to? Or later, when in the middle of crisis I share to some extent his tension and terror? Or, later still, when he has resisted all attempts to crush him? Can we go on pretending that we are like him here too? Are both freedom and redemption on the far side of endurance? Do we really believe all this? Or do we only wish we could? For that matter, do we think that life is so difficult that the crises of thrillers fairly represent our inner responses to it? There are no final answers here. If nobody knows me, neither do I know myself.

An easy way out would be to say that the thriller is one way man has to vent his inner turmoils, his desires, and his fears. The reader will have to sort out for himself the meaning of his discomfort and uneasiness on the one hand, and his pleasure on the other, also the proportion of detachment and emotional participation. Obviously the thriller often cuts underneath our controlled and conscious commitments, and reminds us of experiences that have been denied to us. Just as obviously, the thriller reminds us that our own lives are not usually rolled up into one tight emotional ball, the unraveling of which could solve major world problems. More than any other genre, the thriller invites us to spread the untidy contents of our subconsciousness on the same floor with our approved attitudes, and decide which we want to take seriously.

We all have some sort of cover, the endless, soundless blare of consciousness, to say nothing of specific expectations and memories, hopes and desires, inhibitions and habits. We know ourselves and are known by these. Much of what we are aware of we refuse to make known to most of the people we meet. Some, like Dashiell Hammett, are unwilling to share with anyone all they know of themselves. Most people are more than willing to let themselves be known to someone else. The irony is that we all know so much less than we think, and often know the things that matter least. We are covered by ignorance as well as pretense, and what we do know or fear we know, we do not always accept. And so it happens occasionally that a man or woman is brought up sharp by the realization that he has been living with someone, himself, whom he really does not know at all. "How can anyone prove who he really is? I can't. Do I know myself who I am? That is the terrifying discovery I have made while under arrest: I have no words for my reality."[16] This experience of the self as empty, nameless, rudderless is for some people precisely what impels them to read thrillers. In that reading they will be given one more, and a very special, chance to choose themselves. "It is," as Kierkegaard said, "so hard to choose oneself, because in this choice absolute isolation is identical with the most profound continuity."[17] We must be sure of that continuity if we are to bear the isolation.

We should not condemn those who have no taste for adventure. They are not unreasonable. For adventure, the more free and open it is, cannot avoid situations of crisis. Exhilaration is transformed into tension and fear, and sympathy with the whole world into isolation. The ideal adventure is one in which two meet the crisis together, or two meet each other for the first time. "They had gone from one conspiracy into still another; it had drawn them into the intimacy of people trapped together underground or in an elevator between floors."[18] Most crises are solved better by two than by one, unless one is weak or careless. Apart from what is obvious, we may think also of the intimacy of one person with another that comes as a miraculous discovery at the center of adventure, and which alone justifies the torment. For a reader, even when his thriller does not show him two people in some new union, there is the satisfaction of feeling at one with himself for the time it takes him to lay his life alongside the life of the book's hero. St. John of the Cross' poem, "The Dark Night of the Soul," has been taken as a symbol of so many kinds of experience that were unknown to the saint. And here is one more. But his words suggest an analogy, as "one dark night, fired with love's urgent longings," the reader surrenders to his reading, and goes out from the house of accepted self, unseen by any but himself, and with no other light to guide him but the one that burns in his heart.

We have no more intimate and secret relationship to ourselves than this journey through thriller fiction, from the heights of respectability and excellence down into the valley of violence and escape, and then, perhaps, up again to a new plateau of release or redemption or insight. The insight never concerns others only, and sometimes not at all, but rather casts its penetrating rays on our whole existence, revealing the true lines and colors of that which we thought we knew, and bringing into focus shapes and shadows of a substance we never dared to own. However fastidious or embracing our taste for this peculiar genre, here more than in any other part of our intellectual life we can be assured that, sensationalism and shoddiness aside, this is one place where we are exposed to what we really are.

NOTES

NOTES: 1

[1] "The Last Buchan," *The Lost Childhood* (Harmondsworth, Eng.: Penguin, 1966), p. 119.

[2] "The Murders in the Rue Morgue," *The Complete Tales and Poems of Edgar Allan Poe* (New York: Modern Library, 1938), p. 141.

[3] "Let me lend you the *History of Contemporary Society.* It's in hundreds of volumes, but most of them are sold in cheap editions: *Death in Picadilly, The Ambassador's Diamonds, The Theft of the Naval Papers* . . ." (Graham Greene, *The Ministry of Fear* [Harmondsworth, Eng.: Penguin, 1965], p. 70).

[4] "The tale of political intrigue, espionage, and moral anarchism in modern Europe—which has become a typical mode of fiction in our sinister age of *Machtpolitik,* scientific violence, and 'international evil'" (Morton Dauwen Zabel, Introduction, Joseph Conrad's *Under Western Eyes* [New York: New Directions, 1951], p. xiii).

[5] David T. Bazelon, "Dashiell Hammett's Private Eye," *The Scene before You* (New York: Rinehart, 1955), p. 183.

[6] Ian Fleming, as quoted in John Pearson, *Alias James Bond* (New York: Bantam, 1967), p. 265.

[7] "Who Cares Who Killed Roger Ackroyd?," *The New Yorker,* Jan. 20, 1945.

[8] *Existentialism* (London: Secker and Warburg, 1946), p. 19.

[9] Len Deighton, *The Ipcress File* (London: Panther, 1966), p. 10.

[10] Raymond Chandler, *Farewell My Lovely* (New York: Pocket Books, 1964), pp. 37–38.

[11] Interview in *The Paris Review*, Autumn, 1953, p. 33.

[12] Introduction to *The Omnibus of Crime*, in *The Art of the Mystery Story*, ed. Howard Haycraft (New York: Universal Library, 1947), p. 109.

[13] P. 69.

[14] "The Bond Game," *The London Magazine*, May, 1965, p. 55.

[15] *Ibid.*, pp. 54–55.

[16] *The Riddle of the Sands* (London: Sidgwick and Jackson, 1948), p. 38.

[17] *Ibid.*, p. 112.

[18] *Rogue Male* (New York: Pyramid, 1967), p. 37.

[19] *Ashenden* (New York: Avon, 1966), p. 11.

[20] *The Journals of Soren Kierkegaard* (London: Oxford, 1951), p. 213.

[21] *The Secret Agent* (New York: Anchor, 1953), p. 35.

[22] *The Journals*, p. 213.

[23] *Ibid.*, p. 251.

[24] *The Mechanical Bride* (Boston: Beacon, 1967), pp. 108–109.

[25] Paraphrase of encounter between Oedipus and Tiresias in *King Oedipus*.

[26] "The Simple Art of Murder," *The Art of the Mystery Story*, p. 237.

[27] *Ibid.*

[28] *A Murder of Quality* (Harmondsworth, Eng.: Penguin, 1966), p. 83.

[29] Dashiell Hammett, *The Maltese Falcon* (New York: Vintage, 1964), pp. 193–95.

[30] *The Looking-Glass War* (London: Pan, 1967), pp. 165–66.

[31] Greene, *The Confidential Agent* (Harmondsworth, Eng.: Penguin, 1967), p. 100.

[32] From the title of a 1939 Raymond Chandler story, "Trouble Is My Business."

[33] Chandler, *The High Window* (Harmondsworth, Eng.: Penguin, 1967), p. 96.

[34] *The Confidential Agent*, p. 101.

[35] Chandler, *The Big Sleep* (Harmondsworth, Eng.: Penguin, 1966), p. 204.

[36] *Ibid.*, p. 148.

[37] *Ibid.*, p. 218.

[38] Gerard Manley Hopkins, sonnet 34, *Poems and Prose of Gerard Manley Hopkins* (Baltimore: Penguin, 1962).

[39] P. 136.

[40] *The Big Sleep*, pp. 152–53.

[41] Pearson, *Alias James Bond*, p. 182.

[42] *Ibid.*

[43] *The Thirty-Nine Steps* (London: Hodder and Stoughton, 1960), p. 39.

[44] *Background to Danger* (New York: Dell, 1965), p. 72.

[45] *Ibid.*, p. 104.

[46] *The Mask of Dimitrios* (London: Fontana, 1966), p. 70.

[47] *Ibid.*, p. 71.

[48] *Background to Danger*, p. 74.

[49] *The Mask of Dimitrios*, p. 63.

[50] *The Big Sleep*, p. 66.

[51] *Ibid.*, p. 40.

[52] *Ibid.*, p. 154.

[53] *Ibid.*, p. 155.

[54] *The Ministry of Fear*, p. 218.

[55] *Ibid.*, p. 215.

[56] P. 60.

[57] *Ibid.*

[58] *Ashenden*, p. 48.

[59] *The Looking-Glass War*, p. 218.

[60] *Ibid.*, p. 229.

[61] *Ibid.*

[62] Le Carré, *The Spy Who Came in from the Cold* (New York: Dell, 1965), p. 214.

[63] *Ibid.*, pp. 215-16. Toward the end of *A Small Town in Germany*, as in the two novels preceding it, there is an outburst of moral passion, all the more powerful because it has been contained beneath a surface of matter-of-factness. And once again it is a despairing accusation of indifference on the part of civil servants to the fate of people, in this case a resurgence of Nazism. " 'Of all of you he's the only one who's real, the only one who believed, and acted! For you it's a sterile, rotten game, a family word game, that's all—just play. But Leo's *involved!* He knows what he wants and he's gone to get it!' " (New York: Coward-McCann, 1968), p. 346.

[64] New York: World, 1967, p. 39.

[65] *Ibid.*, p. 38.

NOTES: 2

[1] P. 11.

[2] P. 11.

[3] P. 5.

[4] P. 5.

[5] New York: Signet, 1964, p. 7.

[6] New York: Signet, 1967, p. 7.

[7] P. 5.

[8] P. 9.

[9] P. 237.

[10] *The Big Sleep*, p. 9.

[11] *The Ministry of Fear*, p. 111.

[12] *Our Man in Havana* (Harmondsworth, Eng.: Penguin, 1965), p. 10.

[13] "Burnt Norton," *Four Quartets* (New York: Harcourt, Brace, and World, 1964), p. 4.

[14] *The Ministry of Fear*, p. 174.

[15] Buchan, *The Power-House* (London: Nelson, 1922), p. 211.

[16] *Ibid.*, p. 214.

[17] Nicolas Berdyaev, *The End of Our Time* (New York: Sheed and Ward, 1933), p. 12.

[18] *The Three Hostages* (London: Hodder and Stoughton, 1960), p. 858.

[19] *Ibid.*, p. 872.

[20] *Ibid.*, p. 921.

[21] *Ibid.*, p. 876.

[22] *Ibid.*, p. 858.

[23] Pp. 56–57.

[24] New York: Heritage, 1938, p. 47.

[25] *The Spy Who Came in from the Cold*, p. 75.

[26] *The Looking-Glass War*, pp. 103–104.

[27] *The Spy Who Came in from the Cold*, p. 19.

[28] *Ashenden*, p. 13.

[29] *The Three Hostages*, p. 1133.

[30] James Sandoe, "Dagger of the Mind," *The Art of the Mystery Story*, p. 251.

[31] *The Power-House*, p. 235.

[32] *The Idiot* (Harmondsworth, Eng.: Penguin, 1955), p. 220.

[33] *The Flight from God* (Chicago: Henry Regnery, 1951), p. 182.

[34] *Ibid.*

[35] *Rogue Male*, p. 5.

[36] *Ibid.*, p. 8.

[37] *The Ministry of Fear*, p. 61.

[38] *The Confidential Agent*, p. 17.

[39] Elliot West, *The Night Is a Time for Listening* (New York: Bantam, 1967), p. 201.

[40] *Ibid.*, p. 82.

[41] *The Heart of the Matter* (New York: Viking, 1957), p. 119.

[42] *Ibid.*, p. 61.

[43] *The Spy Who Came in from the Cold*, p. 13.

[44] *The Big Sleep*, p. 220.

[45] *The Power-House*, p. 281.

[46] *The Brothers Karamazov* (Baltimore: Penguin, 1958), p. 683.

[47] *The Confidential Agent*, p. 59.

[48] *The Ministry of Fear*, p. 69.

[49] *Ibid.*

[50] P. 11.

[51] *The Looking-Glass War*, p. 102.

[52] *Ibid.*, p. 32.

[53] P. 79.

[54] *The Heart of the Matter*, p. 218.

[55] *Ibid.*, p. 181.

[56] *Ibid.*, p. 175.

[57] *The Confidential Agent*, p. 9.

[58] *Ibid.*, p. 133.

[59] *Ibid.*, p. 30.

[60] *Being and Having* (London: Dacre, 1949), p. 97.

[61] *The Confidential Agent*, p. 106.

[62] Martin Heidegger, *Being and Time* (New York: Harper and Row, 1962), *passim*.

[63] *The Ministry of Fear*, p. 46.

[64] *A Murder of Quality*, p. 119.

[65] "The Last Buchan," pp. 119–20.

[66] Fleming, *Casino Royale*, p. 127.

[67] *Our Man in Havana*, p. 184.

[68] *The Confidential Agent*, p. 101.

NOTES: 3

[1] Narcejac, *La Fin d'un Bluff.*

[2] *Thunderball* (New York: Signet, 1961), p. 7.

[3] *Ibid.,* p. 34.

[4] *From Russia, with Love,* p. 72.

[5] *John McNab* (Harmondsworth, Eng.: Penguin, 1962), p. 15.

[6] *Ibid.,* p. 14.

[7] *Ibid.,* p. 242.

[8] *Ibid.*

[9] *Ibid.*

[10] *Cause for Alarm* (Harmondsworth, Eng.: Penguin, 1961), p. 236.

[11] Julian Symons, *The Detective Story in Britain* (London: Longmans, Green, 1962), p. 9.

[12] *The Riddle of the Sands,* p. 143.

[13] London: Macmillan, 1965, p. 9.

[14] "The Adventure," *Essays on Sociology, Philosophy and Aesthetics,* ed. Kurt H. Wolff (New York: Harper Torchbooks, 1965), p. 243.

[15] *Ibid.,* p. 248.

[16] Psalm 91.

[17] Simmel, "The Adventure," pp. 251-52.

[18] *Ibid.,* p. 252.

[19] Ambler, *Background to Danger,* p. 115.

[20] *Rogue Male,* p. 12.

[21] *Ibid.,* p. 62.

[22] *Ibid.,* p. 139.

[23] *Ibid.,* p. 141.

[24] "The Time of the Assassins," *The Nation,* April 22, 1944, p. 475.

[25] *A Murder of Quality,* p. 153.

[26] *The Ministry of Fear,* p. 95.

[27] *Our Man in Havana,* p. 186.

[28] P. 59.

[29] *The Philosophy of Nietzsche* (New York: Modern Library, 1927), p. 381.

[30] *Ibid.*, p. 384.

[31] *King Oedipus*, in *Greek Plays in Modern Translation* (New York: Dial Press, 1947), p. 364.

[32] *The Flight from God*, p. 68.

[33] *Ibid.*, p. 70.

[34] *Ibid.*, p. 69.

[35] *Ibid.*, p. 75.

[36] *Ibid.*, p. 73.

[37] *The Thirty-Nine Steps*, p. 99.

[38] *The Power-House*, p. 194.

[39] *The Thirty-Nine Steps*, p. 110.

[40] *The Power-House*, p. 204.

[41] *Alias James Bond*, p. 183.

[42] *I'm Not Stiller* (New York: Vintage, 1962), p. 55.

[43] *Ibid.*, p. 54.

[44] Nicholas Blake, "The Detective Story—Why?," *The Art of the Mystery Story*, p. 402.

[45] *Ibid.*, pp. 402–403.

[46] *The Ministry of Fear*, p. 77.

[47] *Ibid.*, p. 60.

[48] *Under Western Eyes*, p. 316.

[49] *The Ministry of Fear*, p. 191.

[50] Greene, *The Confidential Agent*, p. 59.

NOTES: 4

[1] Buchan, *The Three Hostages*, p. 930.

[2] Maugham, *Ashenden*, p. 19.

[3] *Ibid.*, p. 141.

[4] Le Carré, *The Spy Who Came in from the Cold*, p. 130.

[5] Le Carré, *The Looking-Glass War*, p. 182.

[6] Buchan, *The Thirty-Nine Steps*, p. 158.

[7] *Ashenden*, p. 132.

[8] Len Deighton, *Funeral in Berlin* (New York: Dell, 1965), p. 20.

[9] Frisch, *I'm Not Stiller*, p. 50.

[10] *The Spy Who Came in from the Cold*, p. 129.

[11] West, *The Night Is a Time for Listening*, p. 93.

[12] Pp. 110–11.

[13] *The Night Is a Time for Listening*, p. 158.

[14] *The Spy Who Came in from the Cold*, p. 10.

[15] II, 360, trans. F. M. Cornford (New York: Oxford, 1950) p. 45.

[16] *I'm Not Stiller*, p. 68.

[17] *Either-Or* (passage used as epigraph in *I'm Not Stiller*).

[18] *The Night Is a Time for Listening*, p. 60.

This book was set in ten-point Palatino. It was composed and printed by Oberlin Printing Company, Oberlin, Ohio, and bound by The C. J. Krehbiel Company, Cincinnati, Ohio. The paper is Bradford Book.
The design is by Edgar J. Frank.